The Complete Beginner's Guide to Archery

The Complete Beginner's Guide to
ARCHERY

BERNHARD A. ROTH
with photographs
by Edward DeRienze

Doubleday & Company, Inc.   Garden City, New York

All photographs in this book were taken by Edward DeRienze with the following exceptions:

Bear Archery: pp. ii, x, 10, 19, 35, 101, 122
The British Information Services: pp. 13, 17
The British Museum: p. 12
Hitt Archery: pp. 138, 140, 141
Saunders Archery: pp. 20, 114, 116, 121
G. Smith: pp. 102, 103, 104

ISBN: 0-385-07344-5 Trade
0-385-07356-9 Prebound
Library of Congress Catalog Card Number 75–26942

9 8 7 6 5 4 3 2

Acknowledgment

It has been well said that the perfect archer has not yet been born—close as some have come to that ideal. Always, as a complete mastery of the sport seems near enough to reach, some unseen force snatches it away. Bow-people, then, are never quite mature, but forever in a state of growing up, and reveling in a sort of eternal springtime. For their share in inspiring the author to capture scenes from this Camelot-type world, there are a host of merry searchers-for-the-Archer's-Grail to be thanked. Chief among them are Ed and Hedy, Basil and Rose, and Claire, the author's own Maid Marian. At long last, too, here's tribute to the all-around sportsmen of the Delaware County Field & Stream Association, who took bumptious archers to their bosom, and provided them ample roving space amid the rustic wonders of Pennsylvania.

Contents

The Complete Beginner's Guide to Archery

Archery is a quiet sport.

1. Bow-benders, Unite

Welcome to the ranks of the "bow-benders." You're joining one of the largest "families" of specialized sports people in the world. You'll soon be enjoying a common bond with the millions of other archers. In just about every country on earth, there are people flicking arrows at targets of one sort or another.

Your first contacts with the bow-legion may be members of the local archery club. Taking out membership for yourself will be a wise move. This will lead you to places to go shooting, to coaching from experienced bowmen, and to all sorts of information on happenings in the archer's calendar. On top of that, you'll start new friendships that unite bow-enthusiasts wherever they gather.

Maybe you'll begin your adventure at a commercial indoor archery range. Hundreds of these are open seven days a week —evenings, too—in many regions of the U.S.A. Rates per hour are reasonable compared to other indoor-sport facilities. Again, you'll have found a safe, convenient place to shoot, to sharpen skills, and to match your performance with others.

Professional instructors are on hand at many indoor ranges, in addition to well-equipped tackle shops. And you'll be mixing

A good archery tackle shop will help you.

it up with the same sort of friendly, helpful crowd you'd encounter at any archery hotspot.

A good archery tackle shop will also help you step across the
threshold into shooting. Generally, you'll do better to seek out
a *specialized* store, rather than a big mart with a small sideline
of bow-tackle. The point is to get advice from someone who
knows archery better than the average ribbon clerk does.

Bona-fide tackle shops are staffed by people steeped in all
forms of bow-lore. Those we're acquainted with have experts
behind the counter who can help a rank beginner to get a good
start; or they can help an old-timer straighten out a shooting
problem that he or she has suddenly fallen into.

Archer-specialty salesmen will insure that the equipment
you buy fits your *individual* needs. They'll tune the gear and
adjust it to your exact style, a service rarely given in department stores.

For instance, a friend of ours tells of buying his first bow-and-arrow set at a shopping mall. He managed to string up and commence shooting by reading the directions included in the kit. Each time he shot, the string gave him a tremendous whack on the arm. Taking his bruised wrist and troubles to a genuine tackle dealer, he was given almost instant relief.

He learned that the bowstring was too long. This caused the brace-height (distance between string and bow) to be too shallow. Thus, when he released an arrow from full-draw position, the string just naturally flailed his arm, being that close to it. Spotting the mistake, the dealer fixed him up with a proper-length string, showed him the rudiments of bow-bracing and shooting, and sent him off to a fresh, much happier beginning as an archer.

What we've said so far amounts to one basic bit of advice: Newcomers will benefit by sniffing out the "inside" sources of archer information.

Unlike the so-called big-time sports, archery seldom makes the front pages or attracts mobs of spectators. And it goes on rather quietly—except for the twang of the bow, and the hiss-and-splut of the flying shafts—in the secluded forest glade of the field archer, or on the sun-dappled turf of the target range. Locations are not heavily advertised. Finding them and other archers' secrets will depend on your own initiative.

A little probing beneath the surface of your community may uncover a surprising network of sites and enthusiasts. For example, we had a visitor yesterday while we were outlining this chapter. The caller was a young mother whose husband and two youngsters had just been bitten by the bow-bug. How, she wanted to know, could they get going?

With minimum head-scratching and some recourse to our phone directory's Yellow Pages, we compiled a substantial plan of operation for her family. It included: a list of a half-dozen reliable archery dealers, handy to visit and so to examine the vast spectrum of modern hardware; two local archery clubs to check on, plus one sportsmen's club with a live-wire archery contingent; an adjacent county having no less than eleven bow-men's societies offering membership, with programs under way around the calendar; a nearby municipal recreation commis-

sion with parkland set aside for target enthusiasts; a local high
school phys-ed teacher willing to share her bow-and-arrow in-
structional experience; four commercial indoor archery ranges
within easy driving distance, all of them running red-hot daily
competitions—including a schedule for the under-eighteeners
enrolled in the Junior Olympic Archery Development Program.

The young woman went cheerily on her way, with a fair
sampling of archer references that will keep her family oc-
cupied for quite a while. Would-be bowmen in places more
isolated than our Pennsylvania suburb may need to conduct a
wider survey.

In areas where archers seem scarce, membership in one or
several of the state and national organizations can be especially
helpful. Collectively, these cater to every interest allied to the
bow-sport and industry. Most of them issue newsletters, fact
sheets, and bulletins beamed to their members' wants. For the
most part, these groups are open to anyone who applies. The
annual dues are generally reasonable.

A commercial indoor archery range.

If you have trouble trying to find local bowmen, clubs, and ranges, state and national organizations can often tell you where they are. This is because the majority of clubs maintain affiliation with other groups serving wider areas and regions. Headquarters of national associations communicate with archery leaders in other countries, too, and exchange ideas for uniform progress of the sport around the globe.

So the watchword is: "Join a national body and see the archer's world!"

In the chapter titled "Archer's Information Directory," you'll obtain names and addresses of these important organizations. Most have banded together in the American Archery Council. The Council provides vital linkage and communication among organized shooters of all types, and among industry people and commercial operators who furnish hardware and facilities.

AAC also initiates programs concerned with outdoor conservation, use of the bow in physical education, uniform standards for equipment manufacturers, recognition for archery achievements, legislation that improves the sport's potentials, and training to upgrade the effectiveness of archery instructors. In the Council, then, we have a sort of "congress," working for all "brethren of the bow."

Note, too, in the "Directory" chapter, the magazines that offer news for bow-folks. All are available by subscription, and several are sold at the larger newsstands. Without exception, these periodicals are carefully edited and illustrated. They afford a constant "sight-window view" of: major contest results; coming events to attend; new tips on shooting accurately; personalities in the spotlight; adventures in bow-hunting, -fishing and -travel; tests of the latest equipment—in short, every possible topic that space allows, to present a sport brimming over with new developments.

The more a beginner reads about, visits, and gets involved in archer action, the clearer become the myriad avenues open to his choice. Some idea of the broad selection is visible in such specialties as: target archery with its fine traditions, the less formalized field events, indoor competition with its own flavor, professional shooting, contests by mail, stunts and games for fun archery, bow techniques in hunting and fishing. These are just the main headings of a catalog full of infinite variety.

With so much going on, some novices may wonder where to make their first jump into the arena. Our considered advice is that you enter archery by the nearest gate and, as fast as you can, get acquainted with kindred spirits. Your bow, itself, will help you find the way.

In my own experience, I'm convinced my bow long ago took over as my personal guide to hundreds of happy sites and episodes. Looking back now, I see that an early, old bow of lemonwood backed with Fortisan, made many like-minded friends for me—friends I treasure and shoot with to this very day.

It all began at the crudest sort of neighborhood field course, roughed out of a few idle acres awaiting development. I had primitive equipment—so did the other folks there. The effect was instantaneous; it was as though we had known each other forever.

Enter archery at the nearest gate.

We shot at ill-prepared targets with little attention to rules; our arrows shattered on rocks and trees—vanished by the score in the undergrowth; we kidded each other's wild performances, and had one whale of a time. And the bond was sealed.

It lasted even after bulldozers ripped up the area for home construction. Undaunted, we searched out a large (gun-oriented) sportsmen's club that would take us in. On some twenty jungly, up-and-down acres of the club grounds, we hacked out a twenty-eight-target field course. This is much easier said than done.

We fought poison ivy, floods, mud slides, heat, insects and frozen ground. Our first butts were heaps of earth, and clay banks full of arrow-busting stones. Early, scheduled shoots were semidisasters, and our gun-toting fellow members looked at us, understandably, as mighty poor relations.

Biting our field points (instead of the bullet) and somehow recruiting more of the bow-clan, we kept on plugging. Bit by bit, we refined the rough spots in our course, such as replacing earth butts with straw. Standard regulations were applied to our range as we embarked on interclub competition. We also went into demonstrating safety and the full potentials of the bow for schools, Scouts, civic clubs and other groups seeking archery education.

The original range has gone through numerous rearrangements. It is one of the liveliest activities in the club's overall program, featuring every event field archery has to offer. Hundreds of shooters rove through it year-round. No one knows how many tyro bowmen have launched their initial, timid shafts across its eighty-yard practice range.

To the veterans who've nurtured its growth, the facility is a pleasant symbol. It reminds us of countless joyful, sometimes toil-worn, hours we've spent together in those brushy coverts; and it recalls the zeal we shared that carried us far and wide to other field and target ranges, to shoot or witness the singing shafts—all of it spiced with the rollicking brand of humor and good companionship that is archery's very own.

So I insist, the bow led *me*, not the other way around. Given a chance, it will do the same for you.

Take note that this sport has every accommodation for you

"Ye object is to hitte ye marke"

to express your individuality. No other sport has greater respect for the differences between people in terms of physique, size, strength, endurance, limitations, activity tastes, behavioral style, motivation, and so on. As the American Archery Council says in its a-b-c's, "It truly is a sport for everyone from eight to eighty."

Thus, keep in mind that this book discusses how-to-do-it *principles*, in the main—not ironclad rules. Step-by-step tips in handling and activating the bow, for example, are guidelines only. Watch closely and you'll observe contrasts in style, from archer to archer, all the way along a shooting line. We are not stamped out of a universal cookie mold, thankfully; we all must bend to whatever talent and other traits we possess.

In other words, we should keep in mind the essence of what we're trying to do. Roger Ascham made the point memorably, back in the year 1545, in his famous book on archery titled *Tox-ophilus*. Said Roger (approximately): "Ye object is to hitte ye marke." Who can disagree, when all is said and done, that our assignment is simply planting a shaft in the top, scoring spot?

Even as the bow and arrow refused to accept burial in ancient history following the advent of blunderbusses, cannons, rifles and the like, so, it is clear, does the spirit of archery prevail in people everywhere. There are those who say the modern bow, in some mysterious manner (perhaps the "vibes"?) harks us all back to our skin-clad ancestors. So doing, they add, there is an assurance of a common origin and heritage that modern mankind sorely requires.

Whether you buy that or not, the instinct for the old weapon shows in many individuals. Place the equipment in the hands of just about anyone at random, and invite them to try it. It is astonishing to see how often first-timers (after minor fumbling) will nock the arrow, draw and shoot somewhere close to the right way.

Such demonstrations make one want to believe what other theorists of the primitive have felt: that many a child given two sticks and a string would sooner or later "invent" his own bow and arrow—with no coaching whatsoever.

Whatever fact or fancy has induced you to step this far into the archer's inner sanctum, all systems are go. You'll soon feel as much at home here as did merrie Robin Hood himself.

Even a child can do it.

2. Bow-lore, Past to Present

Who were the noteworthy wielders of the bow and arrow in the past? What were their archery successes and failures, in hunting or on the field of battle? How did their shooting problems and discoveries compare with ours today? What did archers of old contribute to the shape, size, materials, construction and performance found in the sleek, potent bow on the present scene?

You can piece together answers to many such questions. Clues are scattered all over the world—in written accounts, in museums, and in the debris of ancient cultures.

Bow-hunting scenes at least five or six thousand years old can be seen on cave walls in Spain. The game animals depicted are species of elk or deer that vanished ages ago, along with the dinosaur and saber-toothed tiger.

Drawings, statues, tomb carvings and hieroglyphics preserved in ruins of ancient Egypt give other clues. They show the prowess of archer-soldiers and bow-hunters who roamed the Middle East forty centuries before the Christian Era.

*An ancient bow-hunting scene
from the "Cave of Horses"
near Albocacer, Spain.*

In the Bible are many bow-and-arrow episodes. One of the most famous appears in the First Book of Samuel. It concerns the struggle for the throne of Judah. When the jealousy-crazed King Saul set out to kill David (pretender to the throne), Jonathan warned David to flee by shooting three arrows as signals. David escaped. Becoming king, later, David gave orders that the "Song of the Bow" be taught to the people of Judah. The song ends: "The bow of Jonathan turned not back, nor did the sword of Saul return unsated. How are the mighty fallen, and the weapons of war destroyed."

At the beginning of Europe's Dark Ages, savage archers on horseback swept in from Mongolia and all but wiped out the centers of culture and learning. This happened during the sixth and seventh centuries. It occurred again in the 1200s when the legendary Genghis Khan set out to become emperor of the world. His swift bow-marksmen on ponies shot their way to the gates of Europe, just short of final victory.

Even earlier in time, and farther west, the Vikings, with bow and axe in hand, took over what are now the British Isles. They, in turn, were driven off by superior Saxon bowmen who invaded the islands from across the North Sea.

One of the superior Saxon bowmen—a detail from "a Saxon defending his home"—inscribed on a whale-bone casket dating from the eighth century.

Then came a horde of Normans from the coast of present-day France. They were led by William the Conqueror, said to have been a giant in strength and skill among archers of all time. The Battle of Hastings, between Saxons and Normans, was decided amid storms of arrows loosed by the opposing armies. It ended when King Harold of England was fatally ar-row-shot in the eye, whereupon the Saxons withdrew. The invasion of Britain had succeeded.

This archery epic of the year 1066 was embroidered into a pictorial wall tapestry by the women of Bayeux, France. Visible to this day are the stalwart bow-benders on foot, and the lance- and shield-wielding knights on horseback, locked in a panoply of combat. The tapestry is two hundred feet long.

A detail of the ancient Bayeux Tapestry showing the advancing Norman archers.

The three following centuries saw the rise of the bow as England's national weapon. British kings required able-bodied males to own bows and practice regularly. By the start of the Hundred Years' War between England and France, the English had evolved their formidable six-foot-and-more longbow, shooting "clothyard shafts." Enter, here, the tales of Robin Hood.

Thousands of Robin's kind proved the deadly efficiency of their weapons and skill in battles fought on land and sea. Outnumbered in a series of major engagements at Crécy, Poitiers and Agincourt in France, still the archer-yeomen triumphed. By this time, the mid-1300s, the English were exchanging arrows with enemy troops shooting then-new crossbows and even a few cannons.

The old longbow was gradually forced to give ground to the newer weapons.

Crossbows were never as highly respected as longbows. They gained favor because they required less training to shoot. Meanwhile, the long-range hitting power of firearms ushered in the growing supremacy of gunpowder.

One of Robin Hood's men.

The author with his longbow.

Sport-loving King Henry the Eighth of England (he of the many wives) tried to keep longbow practice alive by law and regulation. He failed, by and large, but with one notable success. It was he who hired Oxford University professor Roger Ascham to write the archery handbook, *Toxophilus*. Reprinted over and over down through the years, his advice is still useful four hundred years later.

During these past four centuries the spirit of the bow has flickered like a candle flame in the wind. It has been near blowing out once and for all among the developing nations.

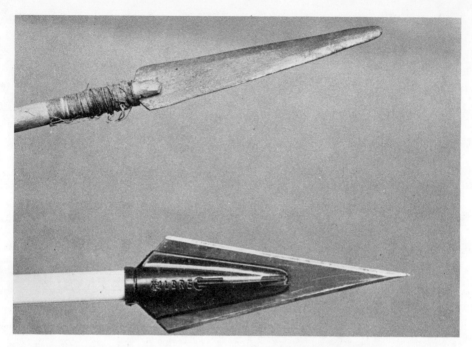

The Sioux Indian War arrowhead dates back to the days of Custer's Last Stand and compares with the modern, two-bladed hunting broadhead below.

American Indian bowmen, of course, used feathered shafts. Although they adopted firearms to some extent, Indians used archery to fight off the conquest of their lands to the very end. In June 1876, they massacred Colonel George Custer's cavalry at Little Big Horn. Many a trooper fell before the short, lethal bows wielded by hard-riding Sioux tribesmen.

Issuing of archery gear for U. S. Army tactical use was proposed several times over the years, beginning with the American Revolution. Army historians say this was never carried out. ·

In Belgium, during World War II, a Scottish Captain, Jack Churchill, was credited with attacking German troops on night patrol, using his personal (non-GI) 100-pound yew longbow. The results were uncertain.

Rumors have persisted that Allied troops and guerrilla units made arrow assaults on the Japanese in Burma and New Guinea, and on the Nazis in Europe. No one has found proof of these actions.

There are records that American forces experimented with crossbow-type weapons having rubber catapults. These were to be used by commandos and rangers in hush-hush, behind-the-lines missions. All the evidence indicates the devices never saw combat.

So, for a long period after Henry the Eighth's valiant attempts to save it, the bow received little attention in the spread of Western civilization. Precious few paid homage to its historic meanings. A handful of Scottish and English military societies continued to hold archery contests. These were largely for ceremonious tradition, rather than serious archery development. Similarly, in the U.S.A., the United Bowmen of Philadelphia were remarkable in their regular devotion to bow-shooting as a mainly sociable affair for thirty years prior to the Civil War.

Thrown on the scrap heap by the military and widely treated as a society toy, the bow's future showed no promise. Two brothers from the state of Georgia did much to brighten the horizon. Maurice and Will Thompson roamed the Florida Ever-

A Scots bowman.

glades, following Confederate Army service, living on a diet of game shot with their Indian-style bows and arrows. Their day-by-day progress as bow-hunters, published in *The Witchery of Archery,* was widely read and discussed.

Clubs were formed to resurrect the old weapon and re-examine its sporting possibilities. Interclub tournaments were held, modeled after those of the Middle Ages. Public interest stimulated moves to organize the National Archery Association in 1879, aided by the influence of the Thompson brothers.

NAA thus began a century of promoting and regulating competitive bow-shooting—a record of continuity rarely equaled in the world of sport.

Archery took another giant step toward recovery in the early 1900s. There was a near-miraculous encounter between a California physician, Saxton Pope, and a sickly Indian named Ishi, survivor of a tribe that had all but died out in a remote mountain hideaway.

The bow-enthusiastic Doctor persuaded Ishi to show him primitive secrets of stalking and arrowing game. The Indian was by no means a keen target marksman with his rough tackle. But he demonstrated uncanny ability to snake in close and pick off live quarry. Pope soon put his new-found learning into practice.

Teaming up with a sportsman friend, the Doctor set about improving bows, arrows and techniques for hunting. Then Pope and his associate, Art Young, began journeys to wild places situated throughout half the globe. In their travels, the bowmen bagged some of the largest and wariest game animals in Alaska, atop the Rocky Mountains of the West, and in the heart of Africa.

They wrote colorful stories and took exciting movies of great animals falling to their well-placed shots. These accounts whipped up ardor among sportsmen. A fever to go hunting in the manner of Pope, Young, Ishi, and other primitive stylists, spread across the country.

State after state responded in the 1930s amd 1940s by passing laws allowing use of the bow in hunting and fishing. Hampered by lack of long-range killing power and the noisier operations of gun-hunters, archers soon managed to wangle their own

A bow-hunter's camp.

exclusive special seasons. They also won a number of archers-only preserves, due to the less disturbing nature of their method.

These bonuses drew thousands to the bow-world very rapidly; the parade of "recruits" has gotten bigger each year since the early 1950s. Of those motivated by hunting mainly, many use both bow and gun, each in its legal period. The taking of a single large game animal, per year, per hunter, no matter what weapon, is a common limitation imposed to stop "game hogging."

In response to the crying need for realistic bow-hunting practice, a group of Californians, inspired by Pope and Young, began developing field-range courses. Allowing ample exercise for "make-believe" hunting, field courses proved just what the arrow-Nimrods were looking for. Many target-style archers, too, welcomed this lively expansion in their sport.

Hundreds of new hunter-bowman clubs and the spread of local contests led to the first nationwide tournaments in field archery, and formation of the National Field Archery Association in 1946.

Swarms of new field-bow enthusiasts brought courage to the few and generally small companies in the archery trade. On hand at last was a fair-sized, clearly growing market—a lively bunch of shooters pleading for suitable bow-and-arrow hardware. They also clamored for special goods and services. Field archers wanted all sorts of specialties for their brand of the sport, items for their roving, free-wheeling, all-weather-active, shooting lifestyle.

An archery field course.

Now we have better equipment.

Bow- and arrow-making firms and related industries plunged into an epoch of technical progress and productivity. New records in output and the general archery economy have been broken annually for more than twenty years.

The fact that the industry now constantly makes *better,* as well as more, equipment shows in scores for various standard contests. Shooters' scores creep steadily higher toward incredible levels, with no sign yet of hitting a ceiling.

If, in some magical way, all firearms suddenly vanished, there would remain the capability of assembling some of the most formidable armies of archers of all time. Troops would be splendidly equipped bowmen fully able to outshoot the best marksmen who ever followed the banners of Genghis Khan, William of Normandy, Richard the Lion-Hearted, and their like.

As fast and as furious as its recent development has been, the bow, as of this moment, shows ample signs of its ancient lineage. Many models made ten and twenty years ago are still around, and well worth examining for an insight on how bows evolved.

Ed DeRienze and part of his collection.

For example, Ed DeRienze, veteran archer and photographer for this book, has collected and kept more than twenty bows having various significant pedigrees. Scrutinizing and reflecting on them, one by one, amounts to an archer's stroll down memory lane:

One is a replica of the English longbow of the Middle Ages. It's one of many produced of lemonwood for summer camps and phys-ed classes a couple of decades ago. It has slim, rounded cross-sections in the limbs, no arrow rest, but has tips suggesting staghorns. When braced and tied by timber hitch to fistmele height, it delivers thirty pounds of thrust via the flax-linen string.

Ed has another lemonwood with flat, wide limbs, in the American Indian tradition. This five-foot-four-inch model was designed to give a hunter forty pounds of push. But you can't depend on it, because the lemonwood gets tired and loses strength.

Most interesting are Ed's several, made-by-his-own-hand models fashioned of yew and osage orange. The natural, rich warmth of the woods adds to a classic appearance. Light in weight, tough and resilient, yew was the most sought-after species in the days of all-wood bows. It stood up to prolonged shooting. Osage, too, was durable.

Lesser-grade wooden bows, made of ash and hickory, are also in Ed's assortment. Typical of their particular species of wood, they show definite signs of fatigue—staying bent from hard usage.

Some of Ed's hand-made models.

The more recently made bows in Ed's array reveal features that indicate oncoming trends. You observe the growing use of backings and facings of earlier synthetic fibers, used to add strength and stability to the basic bow-woods.

You can see designers' progressively greater concern for the handle section, as the older models evolve toward the present. Grips become sturdier, fortified with extra material, contoured for bow-hand comfort. Modest-sized arrow shelves begin to appear, as inserts, in the midsection handle wrappings. Other protective inserts now occur more commonly, where the arrows slap past the bow.

All at once, the chronology in Ed's bows leaves all-wood models in limbo. Here come some of the earliest examples of the current line of composite units. The first of these is slim-limbed, very like the old English longbow, and it includes

Some of Ed's more recently made bows.

a layer of aluminum in its laminated construction. This metal
eventually showed signs of fatigue and was abandoned. A later
model introduces fiberglass backing, a maple core and a walnut
facing. Limbs are still slender and tapered. The unstrung bow
curves slightly forward from absolute, straight configuration.
Both early composites have synthetic strings and exhibit still
wider shelving for arrows.

Finally, there's a model fresh off a modern production line.
Limbs are fiberglass on the back and facing, containing a
hardwood core. The handle section is built up and husky,
allowing a very wide, deep arrow shelf and spacious sighting-
window. The pistol-style grip is the ultimate sculpting in hand
comfort for hour after hour of shooting.

The cutaway at the handle in Ed's newest bow is even roomy
enough to allow arrows to pass through deeper than the cen-
terline. An adjustable arrow plate can be added. There are
fittings for mechanical sights, a bow-quiver, a fishing reel, stabilizers and counterweights—whatever the archer selects. Al-
together, it's a triumph of Space Age materials, manufacture
and precision engineering.

Has the ultramodern composite, sleek with its just-out-of-
the-box finish, left the ideas of the ancient bowyers far and
away in the dust?

Ed doesn't think so. He says, "See those beautiful reflex-
recurve lines in the limbs that turn on the extra power? That
design started in the horn-and-sinew bows of the Middle East,
who knows how many centuries ago. The Turks kept that idea
alive into recent times . . .

". . . And notice how wide and flat these limbs are. I'd
credit that method to the good old American Indian, although
others undoubtedly used it. Flat limbs are easiest to make and
simpler to arrive at, whatever bow-power you desire . . . Nowa-
days we've achieved the miracle materials and processing. But
I still recognize the ingenuity of old-time craftsmen in every
new bow I pick up."

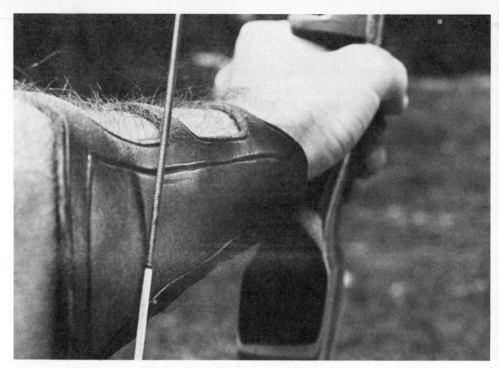

Be sure you have an armguard.

A shooting tab.

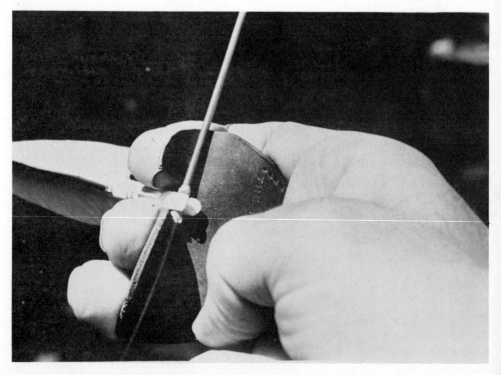

3. Step to the Shooting Line

Time for us to pick up bows and head for the practice range.

In our imagination, perhaps we'll be followed by the ghosts of archers down through the centuries: Robin Hood and his lusty bowmen, the dreaded pony-mounted archers of Genghis Khan, the sharpshooting maidens among the mythical Amazon tribe of warrior women. Their wraiths may well be peering critically at your every shot.

First, let's see to your needs for this first session. What you wear has some importance. For instance, the garb should allow free arm and shoulder movement. Avoid jackets or shirts that bulge out and snag your string. Away with hound's-ear collars that the wind will blow up over your eyes. Catch long hair in a headband, beret, turban, Peter Pan cap, or any other fancy that keeps the locks out of your face.

The bow, of course, heads the shooting hardware. Now for the matched set of arrows—take four at least; six would be better; a dozen, just in case, if available. Next, a quiver to hold your shafts, and a tassel attached to wipe shafts clean of dirt, moisture and range litter.

For your bow-arm, include an armguard to ward off an accidental slap of the string. To save wear and tear on string fingers, you'll want your shooting glove or a tab. And that wraps up the basic weaponry to start. You'll add accessories later in your career.

Shooting at fifteen yards.

One other matter concerns us, since it's an informal range we're going to. We'll have to bring along our own target face and butt, or "arrow-stopper." For the latter, let's use a simple affair, a grocery carton solid-packed with newspapers. We won't worry about "official" target faces for now. Take a handful of white paper plates, eight to ten inches in diameter.

Our first move at the practice area is to place the target in a safe position. This means we want at least twenty yards of space clear in back of the target, and ten yards, likewise, to either side—space where no living thing might come wandering in unobserved. We check the area too for rocks, logs and brush that "chew up" arrows or else send them caroming off into the unknown.

With our target safely sited, the plate pinned to the butt, we pace off a modest distance. Let's take fifteen yards, the starting range for the Junior Olympic archer's program. The idea is to sharpen your skill and learn your bow's behavior at close range. There, your chances of hitting the target face are best. Be not dismayed: It's not unheard of for novices to progress by successful stages to the middle distances (thirty to forty yards) after several weeks of concentrated practice.

We've established our shooting line. We're ready for action.

Straddle the line in an easy stance, the shoulder of your bow-arm aimed in the direction of the target.

Holding your bow parallel with the ground, select an arrow and nock it at the fixed nocking point on the string, with the cock feather (odd color) facing you—that is, the cock feather protruding away from the bow. Lay the shaft upon the arrow rest in your bow's handle section. Steady it with a forefinger as you move your other hand to the draw position.

Readying for the draw, place your index finger above the nock, on the string, your second and third fingers just below the nock. The string will lie approximately in the top joint of each finger. Fingers may barely touch the arrow nock, but should not pinch it.

Place your index finger above the nock, and your second and third fingers just below the nock.

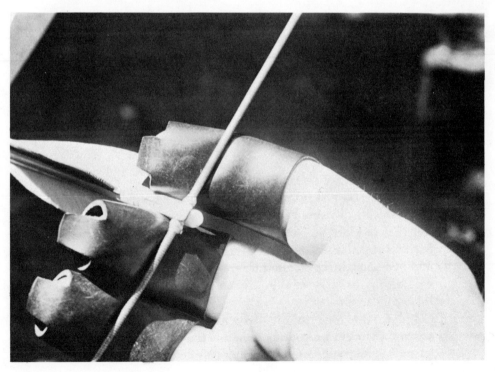

Addressing the target. *The bow is raised to aiming position.*

With the bow still lowered, you may now "address the target." This means simply gazing down the range, assuring yourself that the lane is clear—making certain an animal or person hasn't strayed into danger. Gradually, calmly, let your mind and eye bear down on the target—not just the paper plate as a whole, but its very center. Concentrate on it throughout the following actions.

Rotate the bow to the vertical, bracing it, as you draw, against the heel of your bow-hand; that's the "groove" at the base of your thumb. In a continuous movement, raise the bow

The target-style anchor.　　　　　　*The field-archer-style anchor.*

to an aiming position as you continue pulling to full draw, straight back, the elbow of your drawing arm held high and kept there and locked finally by the muscles between your shoulder blades. Feel that tension in your back as you come to anchor.

The anchor is the exact spot on your face to which you draw for accurate aiming. In target style, the string is brought to lie down the middle of your nose and chin, with your draw-fingers snugged thus underneath your jaw. Field-archer style, you draw to anchor at the very corner of your mouth.

Take your choice, bearing in mind that the closer the bowstring is aligned to your aiming eye, the less will be the chance of error.

Anchored precisely, you'll aim with both eyes open if you elect to shoot the bare-bow, or "instinctive," method. Here, the same remarkable senses come into play as when you throw a ball: Your eyes absorb a picture and send a message to your muscles, telling them at which angle to hold the bow and when to shoot. You must memorize the right picture for each distance shot.

Aiming with a mechanical sight, you close one eye. Your "master" eye takes over. With your sight previously set for the fifteen-yard range, you adjust your bow's position until the sighting pin's head comes to rest directly on the spot you want to hit.

Close one eye in aiming with a mechanical sight.

Maintain a relaxed stance.

All right, you've drawn full length and locked. You're anchored and holding steady on the aim. To send the shaft straight to the mark, you simply *relax everything as abruptly and completely as you can.* In split-second action, the string speeds away from uncurled fingers, comes to a twanging halt that sends vibrations up your bow-arm; you may hear a faint whisper of feathers passing through the sight-window; then, silence, punctuated by the arrow's impact on the butt.

Maintain the relaxed stance full seconds after the release. Note that your draw-hand wants to fall back away from the string. This is natural, so let it trail rearward, coming to rest on your neck or shoulder. Similarly, your bow-hand should be limp, even to the point of dropping the bow. This is the needed follow-through in archery.

Only now, focus on the success or failure of your shot, whether high, low, left or right, or, mayhap, dead center. Review in your mind's eye what you did on that release. Make a mental note of any corrections needed for the next.

Adjustments in bare-bow shooting depend on your ability to memorize the "sighting picture." If you erred to the left, you must aim more to the right. If you shot high, you must aim lower, and so on.

With a sight device, adjustments are slightly more complex. This is caused by the angle between your master eye and the bead on the sighting pin. The procedure may be contrary to what you'd expect. In brief, you move the pin to the *left* if you want the arrow to travel more to the *right*. And vice versa. If you want the arrow to fly *lower*, you move the pin bead *higher*. And vice versa. What you're doing, really, is using the pin to *push* your bow in the direction you feel it needs to go. Experience with a sight will clear up any lingering confusion.

The sight device.

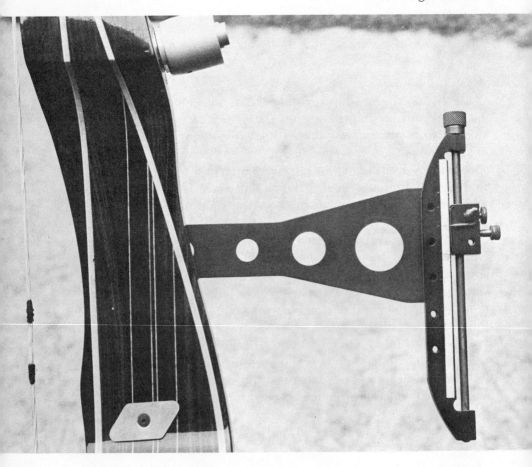

Practice, practice, practice.

If there is any mystic secret to expert archery, the gist of it is this: Practice to co-ordinate yourself and your equipment as a veritable "shooting machine."

Like an engine of sorts, move with deliberate rhythm in every phase of the act of shooting. Perform each function of standing, drawing, anchoring, aiming, releasing and following through, in the same way, in the same amount of time—at least until you pinpoint the need to change, for better scoring. Fit the changes smoothly into your tempo and style.

Since archery is an intricate combination of mind, muscle, vision and equipment that is never absolutely perfect, poor shooting can result from one fault, or several faults, in any single shot.

If you are snap-shooting, steady down.

Improvement comes in detecting the wrongs and converting them to rights—possibly, just one at a time. An observant coach can shorten the trial-and-error process. Try these for size:

1. You're snap-shooting—pulling and releasing as though snapping a rubber band. Steady down, anchor, aim and release without haste. Count to three before releasing. Note the improved scoring.

2. "Creeping" is the way to describe your release. You come to full draw okay, then fail to lock at anchor. Your hold sags forward, you don't get full bow-power when you let go. Notice that your arrows always fall short.

3. You're pinching your arrow nock between your fingers, and you're giving a sidewise tug just before releasing. Spread your fingers a bit, and try to hold straight back until you let your fingers go limp.

4. Your shoulders are out of line with the target; you're semifacing the direction of flight. Hike yourself around until an imaginary ruler pases through both shoulders straight to the bull's-eye.

5. We notice you take a somewhat different hold on the bow's grip every time you shoot. Naturally the bow will veer around, according to your hold. Pivot the bow always in the same "slot" in your palm. Remember the "shooting machine" concept.

6. Beware the perils of "canting" your bow, another word for tilting it this way and that. Field-style (hunting) archers may use a very slight cant away from the arrow rest when shooting without sights, and get away with it at close ranges. The practice leads to serious error when using mechanical sights. Holding the bow vertical insures uniform accuracy.

Enough, then, for this first session. A couple of hours have gone fleetly by. You've shot "ends" of four arrows per stance to simulate field-course shooting, and ends of six arrows as you would in a target event. You've learned that that number of arrows is sufficient to account for when they stray away from the butt as they often do.

That paper-plate target has suffered a number of perforations, your reward for slightly aching muscles in your arms and shoulders.

Make note of how you did this fine first day. Remember, for the next session out on the range: The person you are actually competing with is yourself. Resolve to top that inner person in the upcoming rounds.

Here is your reward.

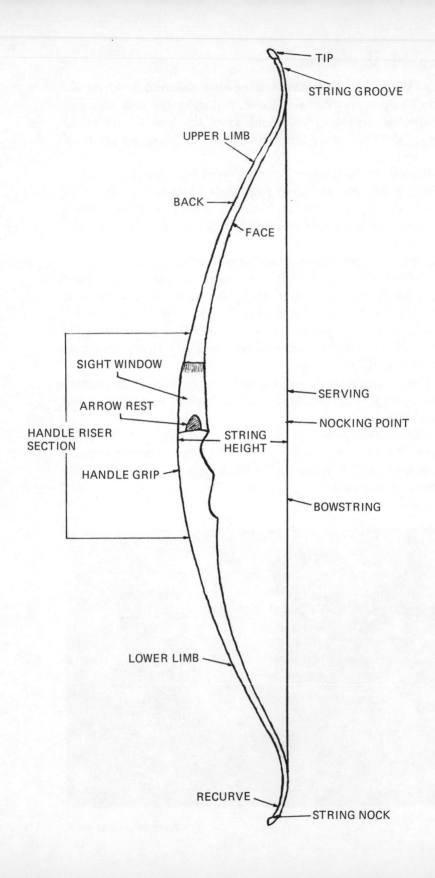

TIP

STRING GROOVE

UPPER LIMB

BACK

FACE

SIGHT WINDOW

ARROW REST

HANDLE RISER
SECTION

HANDLE GRIP

STRING
HEIGHT

SERVING

NOCKING POINT

BOWSTRING

LOWER LIMB

RECURVE

STRING NOCK

4. Bow-shopping

Few thrills in archery surpass the experience of eyeing, buying and trying a new bow. Whether it's your first model as a recruit, or your umpteenth after years of shooting, you'll feel tremors of a fresh adventure.

Merely scanning the hundreds of bows in a first-class tackle shop is adventure itself. Scores of competent firms are busy stocking the racks with the greatest variety of archer-armament in all history. Their sturdy products and infinite refinements cater to virtually any shooter's purpose, physique, sex or age—from tiny tot to senior citizen.

How—in all this vast array—are you to pick the bow that suits you, your level of skill, your immediate objectives and, mayhap, your pocketbook?

Your answer will take shape from a pleasant process. You'll check each bow, feature by feature, for the qualities of performance, strength and looks that match your own ideas.

Most important, you'll eliminate all but your final choice by actually shoot-testing models that appeal to you most strongly. Settle for nothing less.

The functioning parts of a bow and the words used to describe bow-behavior come straight out of archery's age-old language. So pick up a bow, any bow, and learn the lingo. This way, both you and the tackle salesman will know exactly what you're talking about.

Grasp the bow in the middle—in the left hand, if you're a right-hand shooter; in the right hand, if you're a lefty. In most bows, you find a nicely contoured grip fashioned to fit your palm. Turn the bow to vertical and extend it in front of you.

Note that the weapon is made of three main components. The heavy, rigid midsection is called the *riser* and includes the grip. The equal-length, longer components—above and below the riser, are the limbs. Above is the *upper limb;* below, the *lower limb.*

In shooting, the flexing of the limbs and their swift recoil upon release deliver "go-power" to the arrow via the string. The exact design of those limbs—their length, thickness, thinness, curvature and so on—control the amount of go-power delivered. The riser does not bend. It simply provides a pivot point for each limb. An additional pivot point for the entire bow is furnished by the archer's hand on the grip.

Still holding the bow vertical, study how it looks, unstrung. If the limbs lean away from you, archers call it a *reflexed* design. If the limbs sweep back toward you, the bow is said to be *deflexed.* And if the limbs sweep toward you, then curve away again toward the tips, the bow is referred to as a *recurve.* It's the most common design seen today.

The purpose of the curves in bow-limbs is mainly to increase performance. For example, the working recurve is most efficient. Watch closely when a recurve is drawn and you'll see why. *Two* separate areas in each limb will be bent at the full-draw position. Recoiling sharply on release, there is one *extra* kick in *both* limbs to speed the arrow on its way. Thus, the recurve's overall popularity.

Just as a map has a north and south, so a bow has a front and back. The far side is invisible to you as you hold a bow in shooting mode. Call that the *back.* The side facing you is called the *face;* an older term is the *belly.*

Length of bow will enter your thinking, and here's the place to define it. Note that there is a nock grooved into the end of each bow-limb to hold each of the two loop ends of the bowstring. The length of the bow is measured from nock to nock—*along the curving back* of the particular model.

The main purpose of the curve is to increase performance.

Measuring the pressure.

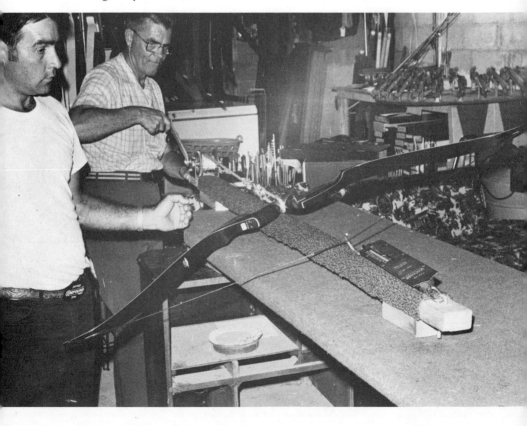

The importance of standardizing the length and other specifications was established by the Archery Manufacturers Organization (AMO). All AMO bows are permanently marked as to length and draw-weight. For example, AMO 56″ 52# means a 56-inch bow needing 52 pounds of pressure to reach a 28-inch draw. The 28-inch figure simply sets a norm. This same bow would scale at about 50 pounds drawn to 27 inches, and about 54 pounds drawn to 29 inches, there being approximately 2-pounds-per-inch difference—plus, if overdrawn; minus, if drawn under the norm.

The benefit of AMO's move toward uniform measurement is clear. Given the AMO specs for your bow, your supplier knows at once the spine test needed for your arrows—and the length and strength needs of your bowstring.

Ask the shop pro to string up—(*brace* is another term)—an appealing model and we'll focus on other important bow features.

Bracing the test bow.

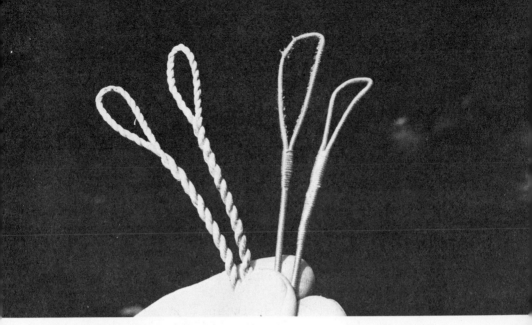

Four different types of strands.

The pro will probably use a modern bowstringer in bracing your test bow. This safe and simple device eliminates the brute strength required in older methods. It reduces the danger of personal injury should a bent limb slip from your hold. A stringer protects the person doing the bracing. It saves the bow itself from possible damage that might be caused by twisting the limbs.

Examine the bowstring. The smaller loop fits the nock near the tip of the lower limb. The larger loop slides up and is secured in the upper-limb nock. Double-check to see that both loops are firmly nocked for added safety.

Close-up, you discover that the string is made up of strands —as few as eight, as many as sixteen. The more powerful the bow, the more numerous the strands. String material is nearly always Dacron, a synthetic fiber, resilient and weather-resist-ant. It is waxed to maintain strength and durability. More strength is added by overwrappings of thread near the loops, and in the string's center section. The several-inches-long wrapping at the center is called a *serving*. It provides rein-forced thickness to fit the nock in the arrow. A nocking point of rubber, thread or metal is affixed over the serving to provide an exact place to hold each arrow shot.

The braced bow is ready for action. Your tryout begins by judging whether the model has suitable draw-weight. Draw the bow to your proper arrow length and hold at anchor. You should be able to hold without trembling for five to ten seconds. If not, the bow may be too much for you. A steady draw-hold is vital to sharp aiming. The idea is to hold the maximum power you can manage comfortably without strain.

Young children adapt to bows with a draw-weight of twenty pounds and under. Teen-agers often draw up to thirty pounds, and so do women target-shooters. Men targeteers range between thirty and forty pounds at the draw. Bow-power of better than forty pounds is emphatically recommended for all types of hunting.

Don't worry if you draw best in the lightweight scale. Sheer muscularity has nothing to do with skill. For example, world-champion women archers draw bows averaging between twenty-four and twenty-nine pounds. Few stars among men target-shooters pull much heavier than forty. This means that their light and middleweight bows are accurate, even at the 100-yard distances often shot in outdoor competition.

How, now, does your trial model shoot? Let the pro introduce you to the practice butt. Clear the range, nock an arrow, draw, anchor, aim and release. What's your verdict? Here, again, you learn to express your feelings in archer's jargon.

For instance, if you were aware of quick-building strain throughout the draw, you might say the bow *stacks* too fast. If the draw went evenly to the full, you'd call it smooth.

On release, if the bow recoiled explosively and perhaps kicked in your grip, you might term it harsh, unpleasant. Such a bow might even be unduly noisy. Ears, too, play a role in evaluating.

Cast is a word that archers apply to the performance a bow imparts to the shot arrow. It includes arrow speed, among other qualities. Actual speed is hard to judge at short practice ranges. Certainly it should be fast enough to lodge the arrow firmly in the target butt. A high-velocity cast makes aiming easier, requiring less radical aiming adjustments for longer-range shooting.

To sum up his or her ultimate satisfaction with a bow, an archer might well say, "It's a sweet shooting bow with a great cast."

Initial test shots may encourage you to buy, but take time to examine the trial bow's other features. Keep in mind the kind of shooting you intend to do. Bows resemble each other roughly; check for less obvious differences that relate to your special needs and standards.

For straight target work, choose a relatively long-limbed model. It will usually offer smoother shooting. This feature you'll appreciate in long, arduous hours on the line. Look, too, for a deep, massive riser section with an extra-roomy sight-window. This will assure ample space for a mechanical sight, a precision arrow rest and arrow plate, and other aiming aids. Check for built-in bushings to hold stabilizers, counterweights and similar accessories. In other words, prepare for refinements you may adopt along the way as skill progresses.

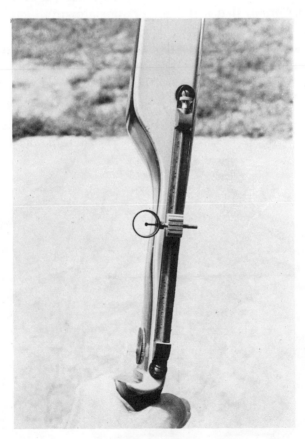

A riser section with sight-window.

If you're beamed toward woodsy, field-course shooting, a shorter-limbed bow may be a better choice. It will be easier to maneuver in the bush or rough terrain, and in awkward shooting positions. For serious game hunting, you'll want suitable kill-power in your draw-weight. But for *simulated* hunting only —"paper punching" around a field course—a target-weight draw will usually suffice. A roomy sight-window will be a benefit, although not as critically important as in target bows. Fittings to install accessories later are also a plus. The riser section need not be especially massive; in fact, a field bow should be lighter to carry than the target version.

Must you have a super-duper, ultra-special bow for each type of event? No, it isn't necessary or required. When shooting for fun or friendly contest, you can use any model you desire. In competition, you can enter with whatever bow matches the official rules of fair play. Many archers use a single general-purpose model for every kind of bow-sport, indoor and out.

The point is that the model you consider ought not to have any *limitations* that may hamper your growth in any aspect of the sport. Be careful before laying out your cash.

Basic materials in nearly all of today's factory-produced bows are the same, if not identical. Limbs are composite laminations—"sandwiches"—of fiberglass and hardwood. Center riser sections are made of tropical hardwoods or lightweight

A bow with laminated limbs.

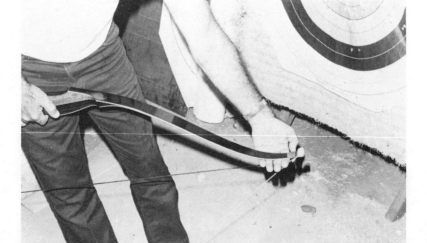

A bamboo bow.

metal alloys. One exception to the general uniformity is the use of solid fiberglass in limbs made for "school" bows primarily intended for instruction. Another exception is the bamboo model—six feet long or better—marketed specially for hunter devotees of the ancient English longbow style.

Similar as materials may be, there are important variations in bow-workmanship. Focus on little things that may count. For instance, a comfortable hand-fitting grip gains in value at about the time you launch the hundredth arrow of the day. Adequately designed string nocks are genuine safety features.

Bowstring grooves installed inboard of the nocks help prevent string chafing and wear, besides quieting the traditional twang of the release. Reinforced structure at the bow-tips saves them from weakening over long periods of use and abuse.

Other bow-facets are more subtle, less visible to the naked eye. Only experience and good advice will help reveal the models that are the result of better materials, finer engineering, more carefully controlled processing, and that will give longer-lasting, superior performance. As with other products, you pay a premium for top quality. Bow-makers stand behind their products. They offer honest, redeemable guarantees that their bows will live up to standards advertised.

Although price does reflect quality, there is no reason to go broke. There are hundreds of very good bows available at very moderate cost. Note, too, that there are often trade-ins and used bows on sale in the pro shops and at archery lanes. In considering these offers, however, it is well to have a competent adviser at your elbow. Be wary of settling for something that almost—but not quite—satisfies your needs.

If you enjoy color, you may be aware that bows are now made in almost every hue of the rainbow. Game hunters prefer somber shades and dull finishes for camouflage purposes. Other archers may be as flamboyant as they like. Aside from adding gaiety to the scene, multicolored bows have a practical basis. Racking your bow alongside bows of other archers is a common practice in all shooting events. Confusion of ownership does happen, however, and color does help to quickly identify whose stick is whose.

Does a fair amount of travel with a bow figure in your plans? If so, be sure to weigh the advantage of a take-down model. You can disassemble or put one together in minutes. Packaged neatly, a take-down is ideal for back-packing, bicycling, motor-cycling—in fact, for any traveling that dictates compact luggage.

The best take-downs offer high and versatile performance. World champions use them for globe-trotting between major contest sites. Some models are quickly adjustable to different draw-weights and shooting styles. Interchangeable limbs can be used to ready the model, at will, for a target shoot, field event, hunting expedition, and so on. Damaged limbs can be replaced simply by installing new ones. A modern "TD" has much going for it, aside from its travel values.

Linger a moment, finally, for a look at a *compound* bow, the most radically new arrival in archerland. The compound veers sharply away from long-accepted bow appearance. This bow is no traditional stick bent into an arc with tips tied by a single string. Focus a bit closer, though, and you'll see that the old bow outline is still there. A block and tackle with pulley arrangement has been added. This merely disguises the centuries-old image.

The mechanical advantage is real. Compounds shoot arrows significantly faster than conventional models—at speeds that improve accuracy. Shooters can handle heavier draw-weights because the compound *relaxes* pressure in the full-draw position. The design, in fact, offers adjustable power settings and the freedom to use arrows of virtually any length.

A take-down model.   *A compound bow.*

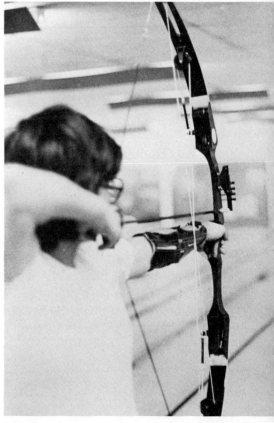

Does the compound bow give you an advantage in archery meets?

Hunters have been the quickest to adopt the compound. Its legality for use in all U.S.A. game fields is a practical certainty. The design's role in official competition events promises to be argued for some time to come. Governors of field-archery regulations show greater leniency toward admitting the compound. And special events for the model's enthusiasts are programed at target tourneys. At the moment, there is no sign that the compound will find ready acceptance at international meets. The basic issue isn't prejudice. The question is whether the compound bow gives the archer an unfair scoring advantage over conventional bow-shooters. Time will tell.

Meanwhile, the "upstart's" popularity is clearly on the rise. Improvements on the basic design crop up regularly, as several firms compete for the market. The compound is relatively complex. As such, it requires good technical service and maintenance. However, compound buyers receive reasonable guarantees. Dealers hold frequent "clinics" to which compound archers may bring their troubles, if any, or their needs for further guidance.

Accessories—including sights, arrow rests and plates, silencers, bow-quivers and the like—adapt as readily to compounds as to normal models. Handling one for the first time, you're likely to judge it a somewhat heavy unit, densely and solidly made. At a common length of about forty-eight inches, it is relatively shorter than the usual bow. In price, it will generally be found up there with top-of-the-line, quality models of regular design.

You probably now want to pick a bow and go down to the shooting line forthwith. Begone, then—we're with you 100 per cent.

Don't be chagrined, though, if some new wrinkle in archery technique develops while you're en route to the range. The advent of the compound is but one illustration of dynamics unleashed in the archer's universe. All signs point to equally startling designs on the verge of springing off the industry's drawing boards full-blown. Archery may have slumbered four or five centuries, but it's on twenty-four-hour alert today.

COCK FEATHER   CREST   PILE

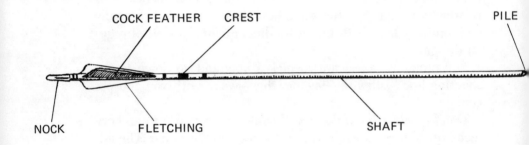

NOCK   FLETCHING   SHAFT

ARROW NOMENCLATURE

This diagram gives the terms used in referring to various parts of an arrow's anatomy.

5. The Way of an Arrow

Keen archers choose arrows with great care. Some will even say, "I can get along with a so-so bow, but you'll never catch me afield with a motley bunch of arrows."

This saying can be challenged, but the sense of it proves out. A grab-bag collection of arrows shot from a given bow will spray all over the countryside. No matter how good your bow-work, unsuited shafts will yaw, flutter, side-slip and otherwise frustrate your aim. Practice until doomsday with them, and they'll just keep on flying wild.

Your hits will begin to pierce the bull's-eye on the day you draw a matched and uniform set of shafts. Arrows should be scaled exactly to your physique, your bow and your type of shooting. They should be as much alike as peas in a pod, each one designed to fly the same path through the air when shot correctly from your bow.

You won't always find the right shafts, readymade, in dealers' racks, or in archery "sets" packaged for mass sales. Stock sizes may be too short, too long, or too something else that will reduce your chances of consistent accuracy. With experience in what you really need, you may get around to making your own arrows. For a starter, we suggest you get fitted at a pro tackle shop. Also, there are plenty of good mail-order firms in the arrow business. But they'll require your exact specifications.

Length is the number-one specific. It's based on your own, individual draw. Actual measuring is necessary. Little people sometimes draw long; and some big people draw remarkably short. So brace your bow at full draw with an extra-long shaft nocked on the string. Get someone to mark the shaft where it meets the far side (back) of the bow. Measure from the cleft in the nock to the mark. This is the exact length you'll order. Arrow-makers will add slightly more length depending on the type of point or head you choose. First, though, they must know the measurement just described.

Spine is another vital factor. "Stiffness" is a substitute word that may help explain this bit of archer's lingo. To understand arrow-spine's importance requires imagination, or, better still, a slow-motion camera.

Try this word-picture: Load an arrow in your bow. Pull to full draw on target. Anchor. Now release. You've set immense force into motion. If your eye were quick enough, you'd see weird behavior in the few milliseconds during which the arrow reacts to the string, spurts away, and passes through the sight-window—streaking toward its objective.

A grab-bag collection of arrows.

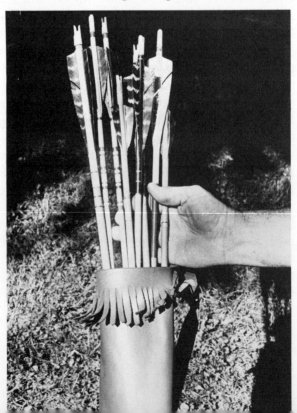

Brace your bow at full draw.

The bow-force you released is concentrated on the relatively small arrow nock. The arrow is *not* in a tube, like a bullet in a gun barrel. Its only guide or support is the tiny area of the rest and plate in the bow. Otherwise, the arrow is free. And, in its freedom, it will bend, buck, wiggle, snake and do all manner of gyrations. This behavior continues for split seconds after leaving the bow, before the shaft settles down on true course.

Carefully selected shaft-spine is a means of controlling the wild motions of the arrow's take-off. Correct spine doesn't stop the bending and wavering. It simply regulates it. Since heavy draw-weight bows deliver strong power at the string, they require relatively stiff-spined arrows. On the other hand, shafts for lighter bows need less spine; they're subject to less propulsive force.

Spine is also related to the length of the shaft. Longer shafts tend to be more flexible; shorter ones, stiffer—all other factors being equal. For a bow of a given power, then, long arrows need greater built-in resistance to bending—more spine—than shorter arrows.

Select your shaft-spine carefully.

On the practice range, be suspicious if your shots tend to veer horizontally (left or right) away from the heading of the bow. Wide-left for a right-hander, or wide-right for a left-hander, may mean *too much* spine. If they err in directions opposite from the foregoing, suspect *too little* spine. These are hints, only. Other factors may need checking, too.

Much guesswork can be avoided at the outset by using information furnished by members of the Archery Manufacturers Organization (AMO). Their tables make it easy to single out the precise spine to specify for your draw- and bow-weight. Run your finger down and/or across listings. You'll find they've been worked out to give the specs for each type of shaft material—also for all arrow types, including target, field and hunting.

Three common shaft materials are aluminum, glass fiber and wood. Each is capable of producing beautiful arrows by careful manufacturing. All have rightful places in the complete archer's kit.

For serious competition in target and field shooting, aluminum is often a first choice. This metal affords the widest assortment of arrows customed to nearly every conceivable spec. Aluminum-tube factory methods provide shafts of even quality, precisely controlled in straightness, diameter, spine and weight. They adapt well to the fitting of heads, nocks, fletching and colorful cresting. Although a bit more costly than other materials, aluminum gives long service when properly used.

Fiberglass shafts have also proven their worth over many years. The material competes with aluminum, affording excellent arrows for target, field and hunting use. Except for solid-glass fishing arrows, glass shafts are tubes of precise, uniform manufacture. They adapt nicely to installing points, nocks, fletching and crests. They're amazingly tough under hard usage. Glass shafts are usually priced somewhat lower than aluminum.

Solid wood dowel is, of course, the age-old tradition in arrow-making. Wooden shafts still play a strong role in archery. Well-made, matched sets respond perfectly to the skill of any bowman who shoots them. They're good for target and field—every phase of the sport except bow-fishing. Rarely, however, are they used in the top echelons of competition. One reason is the increasing scarcity of quality arrow woods—especially choice, Port Orford cedar. Also, compared with other materials precision arrow specs are much harder to obtain in wood.

You might select aluminum arrows.

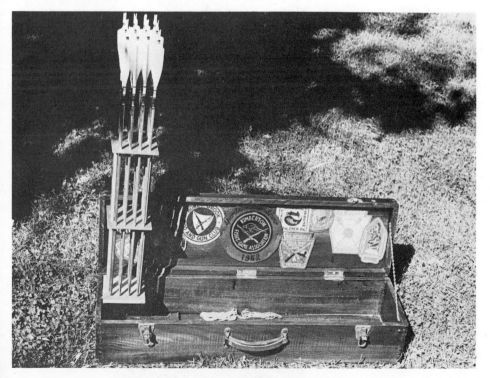

Looking at the three common materials, side by side, you'll find that each has unique pluses and minuses. This kind of shooting you have in mind should guide your choice. Cost, too, may merit pondering. The fact is, arrows are *not* forever. They vanish, self-destruct, and need repair. Over the long haul, arrow supplies and maintenance are likely to be among the larger items in your archery budget.

In terms of *initial purchase only*, wood shafts require the least outlay; fiberglass rate next in economy, followed closely by aluminum.

Thinking of added costs in maintenance and replacement, take note that wood is more likely to break and warp than are the other materials. Fiberglass shafts have supreme resistance to breaking. Aluminum, too, has great longevity, but it will bend and stay bent; the straightening process demands equipment and know-how.

There's a way to save a penny, using tube-type shafts, both aluminum and fiberglass. Fittings are available which allow quick changing of arrow piles (points) and heads to suit the moment. Thus, with a supply of special, extra screw-in heads, you can switch from target shooting, to field, to hunting, in a matter of minutes. The piles must all be of uniform weight, for shooting accuracy. Money saved plus the multi-use convenience are real bonuses.

Quick-changing an arrowhead.

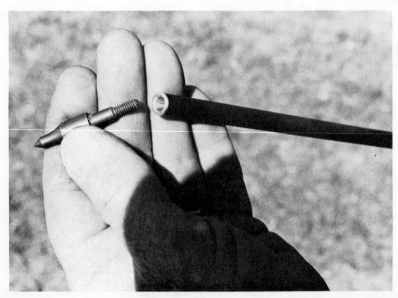

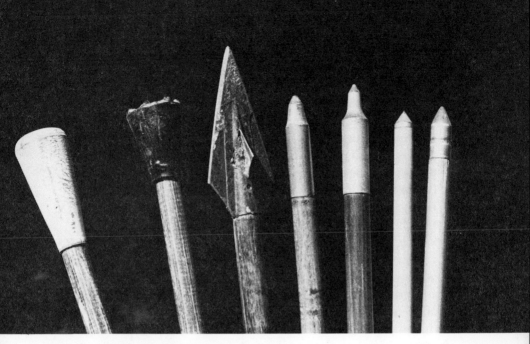

Arrowhead fittings should be secure.

Changeable heads for wood arrows exist. They're harder to find, however, and limited in sizes and designs.

The standard, cone-shaped pile for the target shooter's arrow remains popular. Except for improved metals used in manufacture and better fitting to the shaft, it changes little, year to year.

There's a broader selection of points for field-type shooting, due mainly to the woodsy, bushy, rough-and-ready conditions in which it often takes place.

Whatever the point or head, its first job is to punch a hole in the target face and stay there. It should also be designed to punch a clean "hole" through the air with minimum resistance —meaning that a certain streamlining is effective. Again, the weight of the point must be right for balanced arrow flight.

Just as important as the head itself is the way it's affixed to the shaft. Sloppy, insecure fittings will be a constant source of problems. They'll cause arrows to bounce off the target. Or the heads will pull off and stay hidden in the backstop or bale. Or they'll pop off on impact and disappear. Or they'll create air turbulence in flight, ruining your aim.

Special problems occur with heads on wooden shafts. Heads crimped on the cheaper arrows always weaken the wood and soon break at the crimp line. The glue used to secure points eventually "tires" and lets go, especially on cold days when glue is prone to crystallize. A chronic fault with points on wood arrows is snagging due to overhang—that is, the head juts out beyond the diameter of the shaft. This happens because the fitting goes over the dowel. It can be corrected by a tapered fit, blending flush with the shaft surface.

Arrow points designed for easiest retrieval are of greatest concern to the field-style archer. If you lean that way, think far ahead before arming your arrows. For sure, they'll stab into tree trunks, stumps and clay banks—as well as the target bale. Have a care, then, that your selected points will dislodge readily from all sorts of foreign materials. Some types will, and some won't. Check this out, and carry a pair of pliers for insurance.

Opposite from the "business end" of the arrow is the small component called the *nock*. (Note that there are nocks on your bow as well, the grooves that hold the loops at either end of the string.) Arrow nocks are engineered in plastic to propel thousands of successful launchings. Therefore, they must align precisely with the shaft and assure smooth release.

They need strength to absorb bow-power plus the shock of myriad impacts. Nocks should satisfy the personal, hands-on style of the archer who uses them. Manufacturers offer an almost infinite variety of dimensions and colors. The choice includes nocks with "feelers" to speed positioning of the arrow on the string. A popular model responds to dipping in hot water. The nock can then be pinched or widened to fit the width of the string. It becomes rigid again on cooling.

Attaching the nock to the shaft is as vital as nock design. Nocks joined to tubular shafts by means of special bushings plus a screw-and-glue process give outstanding security.

Forward of the nock, is the arrow's flying gear. The fletching, consisting of several vanes, suggests a form of aircraft or guided missile. Stabilizing the arrow on course, the fletching acts, in some respects, like the tail assembly of an airplane.

A fletching with four vanes.

Fletching composed of three vanes is most common; four vanes are not unusual; five and six vanes are possible.

The vanes are arranged equidistant around the shaft. In three-vane setups they are usually 120 degrees apart. Note that the position of the vanes is related directly to the arrow nock. Viewed endwise, the cock feather (or cock vane) is at right angles to the cleft in the nock. Generally, too, the cock feather is a distinct, different color. In shooting position, it will be the vane farthest away from the bow. It acts as a quick indicator for nocking the arrow.

A spinning motion adds desired steadiness to arrow flight. For that reason, vanes are angled a bit off the straightforward axis. They act like rudders on a plane. Increasing or decreasing the angle speeds up or slows down the spin. A two-degree, so-called "helical," angle is the usual standard. The shaft can be spun to the left or right, as desired, by deflecting vanes one way or the other. Spiraling of a heavy hunting arrow shot at point-blank range may have little or no advantage. Such arrows are often fletched straightforward.

Picturesque and useful as natural feather fletching has always been, it is slowly giving ground to synthetic vanes. Arrow-makers report dwindling supplies of good turkey pinions, the feathers generally used.

Meanwhile, the plastic industry has been rapidly catching up. Their newer, die-cut vanes are soft and flexible—shooting smoothly as feather, but with a tough elasticity and endurance all of their own.

No matter what the material, fletching faces exacting demands. Vanes should offer the barest resistance when passing through the arrow rest on release. They must provide working control surfaces that pilot the arrow in its aerial journey. Subject to ruthless banging around, impacts and weather, they must still retain their shape. Their tenacious sticking to the shaft is imperative.

The design of vane patterns has genuine elements of aerodynamics. Length, height and surface area of the vane are plotted in relation to the type of arrow it will guide. Too much surface is a waste, adding unwanted drag through the air. Too little,

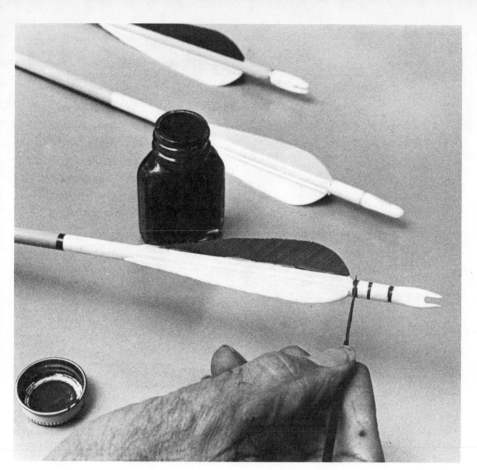

Applying cresting.

and there's a wobbling shaft. The result is a vast welter of patterns and sizes available for modern fletching—the rainbow hues spatter color on the archer's scene.

Cresting—those flamboyant bands and stripes at the rear of the shaft—adds color, also. It serves two useful purposes. Color cresting identifies your particular arrows, and makes them easier to see and find if they wander from the target.

If you're worried that someone else will turn up with the very same crest design—well, maybe they won't have the same length, fletching, heads or nocks. Or, put an end to the problem: Mark the shafts with your name on decals, in India ink or whatever else will stand the abuse. A good arrow deserves a proud owner.

Checking out equipment.

A good shop has something for every archer.

6. Visit to an Archers' Den

Now that you've decided that archery is your thing, I'm going to take you to Del Gilbert's. His shop sells nothing but archery equipment. Every salesperson there is a fully qualified archer.

You find that Del's is a home shop occupying the entire spacious basement of a large stone ranch house. At first glance, you wonder if you've entered the armory of some medieval fortress, or the hunt room of an ancient castle, or perhaps the hiding place of Robin and his Merrie Outlaws.

Yet these are modern bows dangling rack upon rack from the rafters. And the colors of freshly crested and fletched arrows by the dozen line the walls and catch your eye, together with assorted quivers, shooting gloves and tabs, armguards, brush buttons, silencers, bow-bracers, nocking sets, bowstrings and what all.

A wall-mounted deer head gazes down on a long glass display case serving as a counter. Its shelves are loaded with metalware: arrow points for target-, field-course, fish-, and game-shooting, plus an array of sighting devices. Through a doorway back of the counter there's evidence of a workshop, judging by the benches, tool racks, vises and such. In the distance is a drum-shaped table with arrow shafts in process clamped in a circular arrangement.

Your ear suddenly picks up a series of twang, zip, and phut noises that come only from bowmen in action. Turning, you locate two shooters zeroing in at short range on a target butt in a corner. Adjacent are a huge stone fireplace, sofa and chairs, and a table stacked with colorful reading material. Apparently, it's a nook to relax over bow-lore, and a good spot to chat with other enthusiasts.

The club-room atmosphere sinks in on you pleasantly. The hustle-bustle-sell tone of other kinds of shops is entirely absent. At the moment, Del is listening closely to a youngster reciting a minor problem in nocking his arrow. Two older fellows who came in to buy expensive hunting bows join in with their own friendly advice to the lad. No one's crowding anybody.

Minute by minute, you're learning why we came here—and why we advise that you search out a place like it. Most striking to you may be the great amount of measuring, fitting, adjusting, checking and rechecking that occurs as Del and staff serve each individual customer. It dawns on you that the tackle selected is being "tailored" to the person very much like a suit of clothing.

Checking and rechecking.

For the first time, you realize that many factors go into choosing a bow, such as whether the shooter is right- or left-handed; the size and physical strength of the bowman; whether the bow is intended for precise target work, or rough-and-ready field archery; whether the intent is bare-bow (instinctive) shooting, or free-style, with aiming and stabilizing devices to be added; the size of the sight-window, the notch through which the shooter views the target; the desired sturdiness of bow-nocks that hold terminal loops of the string; the comfort or discomfort of the bow-hand where it grips the pivotal point. Some people are fussy about colors and shades of coloration.

You may conclude that there's no end to the choices when one customer asks for a model he can take handily on airline trips. No problem. Del's assistant, Buzz Sawyer, produces a glistening longbow, presses a button on each limb, and packs the bow's three separate sections into a piece of travel luggage about the size of an attaché case. The happy customer departs, predicting he'll be back to buy an extra set of heavier limbs later, for use in hunting season.

When it's your turn to get fitted, you discover there's more to selecting an arrow than simply grabbing a stock shaft off the rack. Del's wife, Grace, hands you a measuring shaft. It has graduated markings, for various lengths, inked on its flank. Nocking it on the string of a test bow, she asks you to pull to a comfortable full draw. She makes note of the length indicated where the shaft extends beyond the back of the bow, the side nearest the target.

Grace remarks that you draw twenty-eight inches, which happens to be used by most of the archery industry as a standard in calibrating equipment. You express surprise at your measurement. A taller bowman preceding you had just measured at only twenty-six inches. Grace smiles and says, "Yes, and that's just why we have to be finicky. Few people think of it in connection with bow-tackle. Otherwise, they know very well there are big people with short arms or narrow shoulders—and little people with long arms and wide shoulders. So, tailored tackle really is important to keen, comfortable shooting."

Your education in arrow-ology unfolds as Grace helps you pick out the right shaft-spine (stiffness) to match your bow-weight, and the best shaft material (wood, glass or aluminum) to suit your intentions and pocketbook. Other special decisions include whether you want target or field points, or perhaps a screw-in bushing that enables you to switch from one to another in seconds.

Then you come to fletching: Shall it be feather vanes or plastic—the more usual three-vane arrangement, or the four-vane which some prefer?

To top it off, what color cresting to identify your own arrow among others sticking in a target, and thus make the missile easier to spqt when it flies astray?

The fletcher at work.

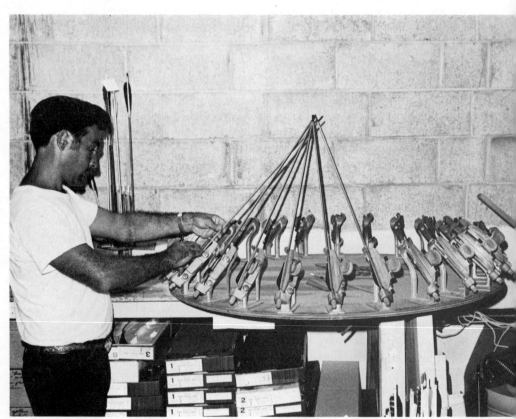

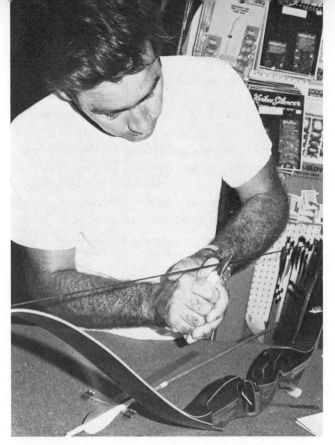

Tuning the bow.

The nocking spot has been found.

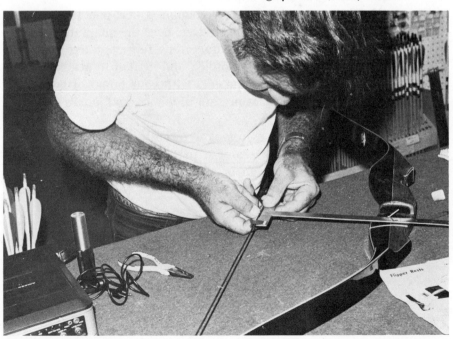

It's deep evening and near closing time as your initial shopping spree at Del's draws to an end. You're outfitted with a set of gear that fits you like a glove: a bow you know draws sweet and smooth from actual shooting at a practice butt—one that pulls exactly thirty-eight pounds according to the weighing you witnessed at Del's scales; arrows that will fly true as fast as your skill develops to make them behave; an armguard, finger tab and arrow rest to insure snag-free arrow releasing; a roomy quiver that puts shafts easily to hand and prevents their fletching from getting mashed and out of shape; and a small tight-woven straw butt to practice on wherever you find safe, clear shooting space.

A highlight of your visit is that your new bow has been "tuned" to give an exact nocking spot for your arrows—a precise brace-height for your bowstring. And your confidence is brimming over with a memorable lesson: the careful preparations needed if you really want to score with the age-old weapon.

As the crowd thins out of the shop, Del comes over to wish you the best of luck at your new-found sport. One night a week, he says, they have a teaching session for beginners that covers shooting progress from A to Z over a period of several months. Another night of the week, there's a clinic for the more experienced archers—get-togethers to analyze shooting faults, shortcomings in tackle and so on.

Del points out that you have bought a fine, guaranteed bow. It will be repaired or replaced, free, over the guarantee period. Also, periodically, the manufacturer's representative makes a scheduled stop. You'll be notified and invited to attend. You'll learn of the latest developments with your brand of bow. You can make suggestions, or present problems, and join in the free-for-all discussion.

The tackle dealer mentions a recently held session of this type attended by owners of a particular make of compound bows, the newest design in archery engineering. Seventy enthusiasts showed up to pepper the expert with questions until one o'clock in the morning.

By now, you've noticed that a little blond girl has been helping the Gilberts wait on trade. They introduce Cindy, their twelve-year-old daughter, whom Del describes as his "boy" and the "best salesman" in the shop. With some questioning on your part, it's revealed that not only is Cindy an archer, she's also good enough to shoot in the state indoor championships, and has an Expert rating in the Junior Olympic Archer Development Program.

Cindy is a member of one of four youthful archer teams the Gilberts have coached and qualified to participate in statewide tournaments.

Cindy.

Speaking of young archers reminds the Gilberts of their concern for safety in shooting. Grace says that one of the first lessons Cindy learned when she was big enough to pull a light-weight bow, was that there is no such thing as a "toy" bow—it is no gadget to play with. Early on, they showed her and her friends that even the lightest bow can hurl an arrow that penetrates and hurts. The moral: Never aim at any object "just for fun."

The Gilberts welcome any invitation to demonstrate archery's potentials to service groups in their community. The most frequent requests come from Boy and Girl Scouts and other youth organizations. Cindy is a member of this show team, with her Dad and other experienced bowmen among the shop's customers, as available.

Del says, "We do stunts like puncturing a series of balloons arranged in a row—one, two, three, four, five, etc. We also puncture them while they're whirling on a little pinwheel arrangement. We'll start two pendulums swinging, with pie plates on the ends, then pin the pie plates together when they meet. We also play a game of tic-tac-toe between two archers, using a special grid target just like a tic-tac-toe board. The audience gets a big kick out of it—seem to think we're wizards. Actually, it's just plain ordinary accurate bow-shooting we're doing. Most people could do the same with several months of serious practice plus good coaching and tackle."

According to the Gilberts, they get the most ohs and ahs from audiences when their shooting stunts reveal what a powerful and potentially dangerous instrument the bow really is.

For instance, they put a stout piece of wooden planking against the backstop, give it a whack with a hammer to show how sturdy it is. Then Cindy takes a perfectly blunt arrow (no point or cutting edge), strings it to her child-weight bow, draws, aims, releases and—blam—splits the plank as cleanly as if it were an axe. The audience is all attention.

Then Del announces he wants to shoot an apple off someone's head, like William Tell did. Are there any volunteers? By previous arrangement, someone steps forward with professed bravery. The conspirator is seated, an apple placed on his head. Del stands and pretends to be sizing up the range and tiny tar-

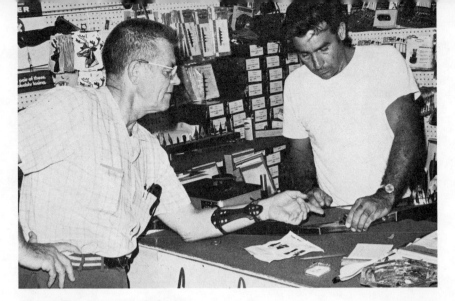

The author gets some help.

get. Ah, no, he thinks maybe he should take a practice shot first. Assistants bring out a department-store mannequin, seat it in place of the human volunteer. Then they put the apple on the dummy's head.

Del goes through overelaborate slow motions of drawing the bow, aiming with the greatest of care and, finally—twang— sends the arrow, deliberately, clean through one of the mannequin's eyes.

A murmur of shock runs through the audience as the message of what happened begins to take hold. The "volunteer" stands up and protests that the deal is off!

That gives Del his cue for a final comment ending the show. He says he hopes that if the group remembers just one thing from the entire demonstration, it will be the act they just witnessed: Fooling around with any bow and arrow is strictly a game for fools.

Del Gilbert's, which is a real-life archers' center in our neighborhood, has its counterparts at hundreds of locations throughout the country. The nearest place like it may be a fairly long haul from where you live. Yet that one trip may save you many more miles of running hither, thither and yon, to assemble all the fragments. Spare no effort in piecing together a co-ordinated kit of tackle so as to be sure that your first move into archery has everything going for it.

Keeping score.

It's almost a medieval scene.

7.   Target Shooting

The urge to prove who is the best shot in the club, state, nation or world has inspired shoot-outs among bowmen for centuries.

Today, calendars of competition are the busiest in all history. Within range of just about everybody, there are events, outdoor and indoor, designed for all enthusiasts to enjoy. Whether you picked up bow-fever lately or years ago, there's a contest somewhere that matches your choice and ability.

You might begin sorting out major forms of competition by attending a *target* archery contest. (The other major form, *field* archery, is discussed in another chapter.)

Target archery is the style most familiar to everyone. Distinct features of a target event are apparent at a glance: the completely open grassed area—the colorful, "bull's-eyed" targets arrayed at one end; white-clad bow-wielders hurtling arrows from a straight shooting line; spectators eyeing their favorites from a careful distance behind the archers.

On a sunny midsummer day with a breeze fluttering the gay pennants atop the butts, your imagination may run away with you. The scene you're witnessing could well be a replay of a medieval target tournament. Let your fancy sketch in some elegantly decked-out noblemen and their ladies fair, a rank or two of knights in armor, and a corps of men-at-arms. Have the white-attired bowmen change into sock-and-buskin, or rustic peasant clothing. There, you've done it. The past of the ancient sport echoes clearly in the modern target tourney.

Note the wide range of contestants.

But stroll along the spectator apron just back of the shooters and look close. You'll see a brand-new world of target archery. Note the wide range of contestants: cadet boys and girls under twelve; junior boys and girls, twelve to fifteen; intermediate young ladies and young men, fifteen to eighteen; and men and women of all ages, eighteen and over. Watch the amazingly uniform style and skill shown as the arrows fly. No rude peasants here. All of modern society, it seems, has taken bow in hand.

Under National Archery Association rules, you learn, shooters generally compete within their own groups. They're classified by age, sex, previous scores, and whether they use sights (free style) or no sights (instinctive, bare-bow). This insures that everyone has an equal chance to win in his or her grouping.

Tackle was inspected before the whistle blew to begin this day's shooting. Free-stylers are allowed a wide choice of sighting aids. Still, each had to prove that he or she had no gadgets not available to other free-stylers. Instinctive shooters are permitted many aids used by free-stylers—except sighting devices. Their bows were rigorously checked. Not until it was clear that absolutely no mark on bow or string above the arrow could be used for aiming, were they given the go ahead.

Free-style archery.

The tournament is in full motion now, with forty-seven targets glaring back across the green at more than two hundred archers determined to show their mettle. The rhythm and discipline of the contest hold sway. At opposite sides of the shooting lanes, the Field Captain and assistants govern the meet's conduct. Their brandished green flags mean "go," yellow flags mean "warning," red flags mean "stop." Their whistles accentuate the meaning of the flags.

Personal safety for everyone is the number-one concern. Aside from the exact distances to be shot, safety also dictates the exact dimensions of the contest area—the allotted zones for shooters, onlookers, officials and potential wild arrows. The number of targets used, too, are gauged to prevent dangerous crowding at the shooting line.

Focus on a squad of four archers assigned to a single target. Their actions give you the pattern. Two of them step to the line

A squad of four archers is assigned to a single target.

Calling and recording the score.

awaiting the all-clear-to-shoot signal. When it comes, they each shoot an *end*—five or six arrows usually, depending on the event or the distance. (They may also take turns shooting two separate half-ends, depending on the rules of the day.)

The other two archers advance and do likewise. Then there is much staring through the spotting scopes at the target until the next signal, all-clear-to-score. The squad, along with all other squads, marches to the targets.

One archer of the squad calls the score made, arrow by arrow, by each member of the squad, in turn. The scores are jotted down on individual score cards by two other squad members—each of whom takes care of two cards. The fourth archer acts as checker on scores called by the Target Captain. All four confer and agree mutually on arrow scores and end totals before pulling their arrows and trudging back to shooting position.

Last to leave, the Target Captain crosses off each hole in the target face, to avoid confusion in further scoring.

Up go the warning flags, followed by the starting blast of the whistle, and shooting resumes. When all have loosed the required number of arrows at the longer distance, the entire rank of archers may advance to the next line closer to the targets.

As they close in throughout the day, you'll see better scoring —more arrows plunging into the center gold as ranges shorten.

The sun climbs and heat waves shimmer over the rhythmic actions of the archers, with spectators peering intently from beneath beach umbrellas.

Minutes and hours tick by as arrows hiss and sputter, whistles blow, and the phalanx of shooters parade to their scoring, and back to the lines. Mounting tension is relieved only a little by the short break for lunch. Word gets around that the leading shooters are matching each other, almost arrow for arrow. A mere few hits separate their scores.

Afternoon attention focuses on the leaders. Hushed groups cluster in back of them, scoping every shot. The pace is telling on other contestants. Typical is one young man whose scoring wavered and worsened as time wore on. He steps away from the line, shaking his head in dismay. You hear him mutter, "I can shoot a great round in practice at my club. I just fall apart when the pressure is on."

There's a murmur of understanding from those who hear him.

This is, in fact, a championship shoot. Winning depends on an archer's nerve, will, self-control, endurance, powers of concentration—many things besides keen skill with the bow. To test these extra qualities, the National Archery Association spells out specific minimum rounds that champions must shoot to gain their crowns. *Round* is the archer's word for a complete "game," as used in other sports.

The tournament you're enjoying, then, requires shooting the FITA Round first, and then the 900 Round.

For the FITA (international) Round, men and intermediate boys have 36 shots apiece from four different distances, measured in meters, as 90, 70, 50 and 30. Ladies and intermediate girls launch the same number of arrows from slightly different distances, that is, from 70, 60, 50 and 30 meters. Total arrows shot by each contestant will be 144. A perfect score would be 1,440—144 times 10, the value of each hit in the center gold.

Bear in mind that a meter is three inches and a fraction longer than a yard. Thus, for example, the longest range shot by men and intermediate boys is just short of 100 yards.

The 900 Round takes its name from the perfect score an archer could achieve if every one of his arrows nailed the bull's-eye. Identical rules govern the shooting of this round by adults and intermediates. This calls for 30 arrows apiece from each of three distances, using the English measure—that is, from 60, 50 and 40 yards.

Somewhat differing rules for younger shooters, and for team contests, are prescribed by the NAA. Extreme distances, for example, are dropped in rounds for youngsters.

For identifying true champions, the NAA points out the superchallenges built into the two rounds outlined above. The combination of rounds compels a wide span of distance shooting—seven ranges, varying from very long all the way down to nearly point-blank.

And the 144 arrows shot in the FITA session, alone, demand a respectable amount of bow-exercise in terms of raising, drawing, aiming, releasing, checking, correcting, scoring, retrieving, waiting, and so on to the final shaft. The athletic side of archery comes to light. It includes miles of trudging and cumulative tons of energy expended in coming to full draw over and over again.

Suddenly the last arrow zips through the late-afternoon light. Flags and whistles send the archers to the judges' table, score cards in hand. A hubbub of discussion breaks the tense quiet of the closing moments. Speedily the judges compare their findings and post the winners and runners-up. As often happens at an event of champion caliber, a difference of barely a half-dozen arrows separate the scores of top rankers in most divisions.

Announcements and award ceremonies over with, the pageant begins to break up. Friends and admirers gather around contestants now carefully re-storing their gear in tackle boxes. You join a circle around the young fellow who was top bow for the day.

You learn that the new champion is only twenty years old. Winning, he out-shot dozens of adults, considerably older veterans of the contest trail. The young archer had caught your eye earlier in the day. For one thing, he wore jeans and jaunty sweat shirt, rather than the classic whites. Most notable, though, was his confident style, the unruffled tempo of his shooting.

He's answering a salvo of questions as you join the circle. Everyone wants to know the young man's "secret formula," yourself included. Many of his friendly replies are technical, a little hard for a newcomer to grasp. You listen with both ears wide open anyway: One of these days these scientific details may come in handy.

Describing his equipment, the champion says: His bow is quite long, as target models tend to be—69 inches, with 12-strand string; brace-height of 7⅝ inches; pulling 35 pounds at his draw; nocking point, ³⁄₁₆ inch above 90 degrees. The bow has a flipper-style arrow rest with adjustable plunger set stiff, and no draw-check. He uses a standard bow-sight with forward extension, single black pin. His single torque stabilizer extends 24 inches, weighs 8 ounces.

His arrows are matched aluminum, cut to 28½ inches, standard heavy points, three-feather fletches with 2-degree angle of spiral, 3 inches long and ½ inch high, standard plastic nocks.

There's nothing really special about his shooting method, the young champion tells the group. He uses the typical under-jaw release, a simple tab for his string fingers. Maybe, he admits, he stresses lining up the string with his aiming eye more than is usual. Also, he takes up to five seconds refining his aim before releasing each arrow. Accuracy goes to pieces, he says, anytime he rushes a shot.

"But you can mess up by being too much of a drag, too," he smiles, as he picks up his tackle box and excuses himself.

There's much to learn, you decide, in pondering all of the day's experience and information. Thrills of the tournament will linger on, plus a hankering to be part of the action. And

A spotting scope will tell you where your arrow went.

why not set your sights on becoming an archery competitor? There are plenty of rungs on the ladder of achievement for those willing to get down to business.

The climb begins with joining the National Archery Association, official governing body of the sport in the U.S.A. With membership comes an official NAA Classification Card. Whenever you shoot in Registered and Six Golds Tournaments, your scores are attested on the card. Your scores will indicate which class you're qualified to shoot in later events.

The idea is fair play, by matching bowmen of reasonably equal skill. The card has spaces for scores shot in the 900, 600 and Indoor Rounds. It indicates minimum scoring levels used to classify men and women. This shows the divisions in which they'll shoot against others of similar ability.

Ascending the archers' rainbow, who knows to what heights it may lead you? Annually, there are state, regional and collegiate target championships—indoor and outdoor. Also, for nearly fifty years, the NAA has conducted a winter league Mail-In Tournament, for schools and Junior Olympic Archery Clubs, professionals and amateurs, men, women and children.

More and more archers are globe-trotting.

Yearly, too, the title of Champion Archer of the U.S. is awarded to individuals having the highest combined scores at all regular target rounds shot, in ten different divisions.

With each passing year, more and more ranking archers are globe-trotting to exotic invitational tournaments in Europe, Asia, Africa and Australia. The prospect of being chosen as an Olympic archer beckons every fourth year.

To many a bowman, acceptance in the Six-Golds Club is a goal for long, patient hours of practice. It's a reward for shooting a perfect end, that is, placing an entire series of the required number of arrows right smack in the center gold. Justifiably proud is the archer wearing the Six-Golds Pin with Golden Arrow.

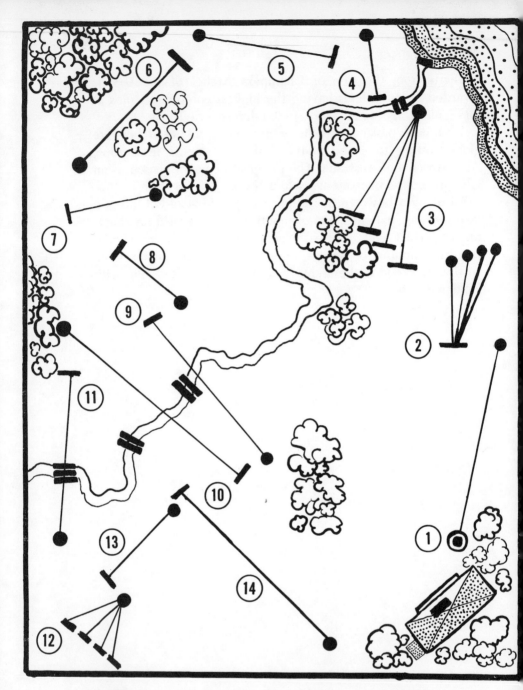

Starting with the clubhouse at lower right, this sketch illustrates a typical, fourteen-target field-course unit. This kind of course, with its uphill, downhill, open and brushy area, affords good hunting practice.

8. Field-range Fun

A little story may give you insight on what field-range archery is all about. Vacationing in Florida, I bumped into some local bow-benders who invited me to give their club range a work-out. I readily accepted and made careful note of their directions. "Likely you won't find anyone out there, since it's the middle of the week," said one of my hosts. "But the targets and trails are all marked, so help yourself and enjoy."

I found the area easily at the end of a narrow back road leading to a swampy elbow off Tampa Bay. The clubhouse was a simple cabin, with no one around. A sign with an arrow indicated the approach to Target 1. I began to shoot the course after unlimbering my tackle, admiring the huge trees festooned with moss, and clumps of giant reeds sprouting from the numerous watery spots.

As I shot and moved from target to target, only the whish-splut of my arrows broke the silence.

Reaching a particular shooting stake, I gazed a long, long way down a corridor of bushes to Target 5. A big gray log lying across the lane looked to be 30 yards out. The bale holding a crouching-panther target face, I figured, was some 25 yards beyond the log. Elevating my bow, I drew, aimed and released for a 55-yard lobbing shot.

I was checking the arrow's flight when something else caught my eye. The log was moving—in fact, it took off like a torpedo, except that it had legs,. a big, snouted head and a long reptilian tail. It was out of sight in nothing flat, crashing through the brush, ending in a great splash as the creature hit the swamp water.

My friendly Floridians had overlooked telling me that their club had an alligator member. From there on, my ability to concentrate on archery fell off. At least, I must have finished the couse in record time.

Field-range shooting isn't always that dramatic. But the unexpected is surely one of its vital attractions. Ranges are designed to test the archer's mettle in judging variable distances, aiming around obstacles, identifying targets, guessing at what challenge will come up next.

Many enthusiasts are drawn by the roving, constant motion of the sport, as compared to the standing-in-rank style of traditional target contests. Often, there's a bonus of healthy, physical exercise involved. Shooting a typical 28-target course takes several hours of hiking, in addition to basic bow-bending. Over rough country there can also be climbing, kneeling, stooping, gully-jumping and tree-scaling, to improve one's muscles and wind.

A confirmed field devotee will scout all the courses in the region just to confront and conquer the endless variety of hazards they present.

Although hunting practice has strong appeal, field archery has a thoroughly mixed bag of followers. Organized shooting programs are set up to give just about everyone the satisfaction of doing his or her thing.

Nearly all courses have practice fields—level, clear areas with targets staggered at various, measured distances. Here the learner can get the kinks out, or the targeteer can sharpen up to his or her heart's content, or the field specialist can tune his or her gear before moving on to the day's round.

Types of events offered are calendared to fit the widest possible spectrum of tastes and skills.

For serious competition shooters, the more formal rounds are

Field-range archery is much freer, less formal than target archery.

featured. These usually have black-and-white targets—sometimes with concentric rings, and always with precise aiming spots. The competitor dwells on pinpoint and tightly grouped arrows. International (FITA) metric-measured rounds also cater to this group, in view of the worldwide growth of field-style tournaments.

For the hunter or average fun-shooter, a fantastic array of rounds are programed. Targets may be any game bird or game animal under the sun, in silhouette form, in color or black-and-white. Formats are often chosen in relation to the season or a holiday—such as pheasant, grouse and quail, as small-game hunting approaches; wild turkeys around Thanksgiving; deer, elk, bear and antelope, when big-game time nears.

Interclub, state, regional, national and international tourneys are regulated by "official" rounds. These prescribe the number of arrows for each distance shot, size of targets and so on. Local archer groups heed the rulings but, on their own grounds, constantly invent new forms of bow-play to make each shoot something of a frolic.

Thus, in a weekend contest, you may find your range livened by a mechanical "running deer"; or maybe a full-size bear in 3-D, sculpted out of styrofoam; or perhaps a groundhog that pops out from behind a stump when someone yanks a cord. Our own club runs a raccoon shoot on a chilly night each early spring. One camp lantern and a large flashlight are the only illumination for each raccoon-silhouette target. Shooting is a bit hairy, and the crowd has a ball.

The voltage of archers' imaginations and due regard for safety are the only limitations on gamesmanship at local shoots.

Men and women, boys and girls are all welcome to the ranks. Sighting-aid (free-style) shooters and bare-bow (instinctive) devotees compete in their respective classes. Awards and other recognition also allow for differences in skill and experience. An archer is judged, then, by his or her showing against those of roughly equal ability. Most clubs set out special, shorter-range shooting stakes for the less-advanced or lighter-bowed participants.

Field tackle tends to be heavier than the regular target variety. Bows are inclined to be more powerful. The heavier hunt-

A practice field on a course—with a fake-animal target.

ing-type arrows have field points matching broadheads in weight. Fiberglass and wooden shafts are more commonly used than aluminum, due to the more rugged shooting environment. There's no ruling on this, however. Any equipment that does the job is admissible.

Dedicated field-range competitors often wield weaponry almost identical to that seen at target-range events. If they're consistently high-scorers, they worry little about bending their pet aluminum shafts around trees and rocks.

Bows with aiming aids are more prevalent than bare sticks. Yet, many field clubs have a hardy nucleus who remain loyal to the no-aid tradition of Robin Hood and other legendary marksmen. Sight-shooters often leave their aiming gadgets behind in pursuit of real, live game. As one of our bowhunter/field shooters put it: "When a deer comes galloping past you, all the frills go out the window."

Targets on a course.

A painted-animal target.

That newer breed, the compound bow, grows stronger in popularity with field rangers. Its advantages in hunting transfer readily to competition. The ease of holding and aiming a powerful model at full draw, the lightninglike cast and flat-trajectory arrow, make for improved accuracy. The design's effective range, in the hands of a good free-style archer, may extend to as much as 150 yards.

Initially restricted to competing within its own special class, the compound has made breakthroughs steadily. Recognizing that the new model by no means "shoots by itself," a number of field groups have taken a local option of admitting compounders to any otherwise fair contest. Only time will tell whether the innovation will gain wide tournament acceptance —particularly in international matches.

Members of a field-archery club.

To enjoy field archery to the fullest, you'll almost certainly join a club. Hundreds flourish, in every conceivable kind of terrain, all around the U.S.A. Membership fees vary in relation to such items as local real estate values, the club's development costs, and the intensity of the shooting program.

Generally the larger clubs are less costly per individual member, having more people to share the investment. Note that an adequate, safe, 28-target range straddles a fairly large acreage. To reduce initial costs and upkeep, groups often elect to settle for a 14-target spread, shooting it twice around for a day's activity.

Some sportsmen's organizations maintain a field range for bows along with other conventional firearm facilities, for shotgunning, riflery and the like. This may make an excellent arrangement for the archer in terms of cutting costs. All shooting sports tend to provide mutual financial aid when managed on a single club ground.

Admission to a club will open the door to year-round shooting pleasure. Your average field fraternity stages a registered shoot twice a month throughout the year.

At registration, you may be charged a nominal fee to underwrite the costs of trophies and course maintenance. Starting in a squad of four archers at 10 A.M., you'll probably complete fourteen targets by noon and return to the clubhouse for lunch. Then, out you go for the final fourteen, rotating back to turn in your score card along about three o'clock in the afternoon. You swap anecdotes of triumph and disaster with your fellow archers until the last stragglers come off the range.

Scores are posted in a hushed moment of truth. Achievement pins, trophies or other recognition go to a few. Better-luck-next-time greets the many, including, perhaps, yourself.

But you've had a wonderful outing in the natural world in the company of kindred spirits, pursuing a sport that very likely enthralled some distant ancestor.

And you shot a little better today—a steadier aim, less creeping on your releases, arrow groupings just a mite tighter. You're satisfied. Still, you can use a few more practice sessions before the next round . . .

9.   Hunting and Fishing

Hunting with bow and arrow is a major sport and means of managing wildlife throughout the U.S.A. and much of Canada. State license fees from bowmen help to conserve the out-of-doors environment. Archer contributions and those of other sportsmen enable game managers to restore once-vanishing species to renewed vigor in many areas.

Added money from sales taxes on archery equipment, as well as on firearms and ammunition, boosts numerous federal wildlife projects. The tax money buys increasing amounts of land needed for game refuges and public recreation. It pays for game breeding and releasing, and for habitat that provides feed, water and cover for wildlife populations. These efforts also shed their benefits on hundreds of songbirds and other nongame species "hunted" only with camera or binoculars and perhaps an artist's brush.

Items of specialized bow-hunting equipment account for more than half of the $70 million worth of archery goods retailed yearly in America. This is just one indication of the archer-hunter economy. A total picture would include myriad other expenditures related to the hiking, camping and travel needed to approach the game fields.

Hundreds of thousands of men, women and teen-agers give bow-hunting a serious try. A small percentage are now and then successful. An even smaller percentage bring home the bacon regularly. A large eastern state, for example, in a recent season, recorded one whitetail deer bagged for every forty-five bow-devotees afield. Few archer-Nimrods attempt the small-game targets, such as rabbits, grouse, pheasants and various waterfowl.

A game warden in an urban county summed it up: "It's generally more hazardous for wildlife to cross a highway than to encounter an average hunter armed with a bow."

All signs indicate that a growing number of archers are bent on improving their "average" in the chase. The challenge and rewards of roaming the coverts in primitive style are appealing. There is no question that the modern bow and arrow in skilled hands can stop any game humanely and with dispatch. The largest species in the world—elephants, rhinos, Kodiak brown bears and so on—have fallen to arrows often enough to make the point clear.

A four-pin hunter's sight.

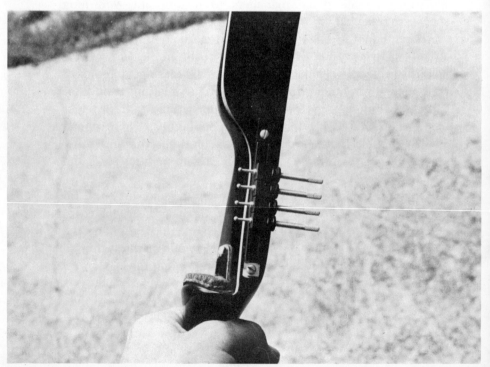

The hunters on a practice range.

What may not be clear are the rigid requirements a productive bow-hunt demands. Tackle, for example, needs to be generally heavier than ordinary target hardware. Certain state laws specify minimum standards for bow-power, arrow dimensions and arrowhead designs. The object is to insure ample penetration and kill-capacity. This actually depends on several factors in combination, including bow-thrust, arrow speed and weight, plus a sharp, strong, hunting broadhead.

It is the sportsman's creed to kill game cleanly. For an archer, this dictates the use of a bow on the heavy-pull side of the scale—something like forty-five pounds at least in a conventional model. Compound bows deliver greater arrow speed at comparable draw-weights. This helps to explain their increasing favor among hunters.

To the stepped-up physical duress of shooting beefier gear, there must be added an all-important requisite for steady accuracy. Frankly speaking, it is futile to pursue game until you can plunge most of a quiverful of hunting arrows into a one-foot circle from a distance of twenty to thirty yards. Since game nearly always offer fleeting, awkward targets, it is well to practice speed as well as accuracy in loosing shots from stooping, kneeling, crouching and other off-base positions.

The minority of bow-hunters who score routinely "pay their dues" in still another way. They study their game's habits as carefully as any naturalist might. Where will it be at various times of the day? What are its feeding, watering and resting patterns? What is its strongest sense: hearing, sight, or smell? They're prepared to take advantage of their know-how, realizing that the quarry, on its own grounds, still holds most of the aces.

High-spirited adventures in mastering the art, science, and skill of pursuing game with the bow, draw enthusiasts to every cranny of the wild country each season. Deer, both whitetails and muleys, are perhaps the most sought-after trophies—with wild turkeys, where available, close runners-up. However, virtually every game species most valued by gun sportsmen— including antelope, bighorn sheep, Rocky Mountain goats, moose and wild boar—are equally prized, and occasionally bagged, by archers.

Obviously, many a bow-toter comes home empty-handed. That most appear quite happy with their lot may be attributed to any number of reasons. For one thing, most sportsmen agree that the essential fun is in the chase, regardless of outcome. Again, there are those long, rewarding hours of contact with the real, original resources of this planet, priceless in a pressurized age. And since many archery big-game seasons are set for moderate weather—in contrast to the gunner's snow and ice —the bow-hunter is usually abroad in the more delightful seasons. Add to these features the quiet, low-key element of archery, and you have a formula hard to resist.

The stuffed trophy exhibited by Fred Bear, Michigan archery man-
ufacturer, is a record-class, half-ton Alaskan brown bear, dropped
with a razor-head arrow shot from a factory-made, sixty-five-
pound glass bow. The equipment, including bow-quiver, is
shown resting against the archer's knee.

Archery big-game seasons are set for moderate weather.

The water-based form of hunting with the bow is called bow-fishing to reduce confusion. Actually, it combines both techniques and is red-hot sport wherever the right conditions occur.

Common fresh-water targets are carp, alligator gar, and other coarse, nongame fish, along with frogs and snapping turtles. By and large across the country, the scaley-plated carp is probably the most popular prey. Their best access for the bowman is generally in late spring when they are spawning and running at the surface of shallow, sluggish backwaters. A loggy-looking lunker carp can give a surprising tussle to the archer who has to "horse" one in. Nailing one calls for quick, keen shooting.

At sea and in salt-water bays, targets are harder to come by. Yet, dauntless bow-folks are continually picking off such species as stingrays, red drum, shoal mackerel, and even small sharks. The trick is to catch the quarry on, or very close to, the salt water's surface.

Fishing bows ought to be fairly "pushy," as you'll be shooting a fairly heavy, specialized arrow that must sometimes penetrate a layer of water as well as the fish, dragging a length of fishline to boot. Forty-pound draw-weight would be a good average bow, and it's best not to take along your prize model. It will get beaten up in swamps or on boat decks. Bear in mind that this is nearly all snap-shooting, very close to on top of your target.

A knockabout bow, a few arrows with fishing heads, and some fifty feet of eighty- to ninety-pound test line pretty well put you in business—except for a reel. Some archer-fishers don't bother with a reel. They wind the line around fingers extended from their bow-hands, anchor the line to the bow for security, and they're ready to let fly.

Reels are easily homemade from plastic cups and other items around the house, or you can select from a wide range of bow-reels on the market. Again, you can attach a regular spinning, or spin-cast reel, to the bow. Either one works fine.

A bow-fisherman in action.

A homemade reel.

A barbed bow-fishing arrowhead.

Note that the line is primarily hitched to the arrowhead rather than the shaft, as a more practical means of retrieving the fish. Of the many designs of fishing heads, the type with reversible barbs has a good deal of merit. After landing your catch, you give a few turns to the head, the barbs move to the opposite direction, and you disengage the arrow easily.

The rubber fletchings commonly applied to fish arrows have little effect on accuracy at the extremely short ranges generally shot. Use them or skip them, as you wish.

When shooting at targets completely underwater, you encounter a problem known as refraction. Your line of vision "bends" beneath the surface. In a word, the quarry will appear to be shallower than it really is. Therefore, you aim deeper than you see. How deep is a matter of experience.

The best practice for this sort of thing must be credited to Keith Schuyler, my friend and fellow archer-writer. Keith anchors balloons, at varying submarine levels, to the bottom of a pond. Then he moves around, deflating the balloons with his bow and missiles—noting carefully the shooting angle required for each—and has himself a ball.

Strange that old Captain Ahab never thought of that.

A modern archery lane.

10. Undercover Archery

Indoor shooting is steadily gaining new enthusiasts as archers awaken to the special bonuses in this dynamic brand of the old sport. Any "undercover" fan will assure you that lane shooting delivers all the primitive thrills of the bow and arrow, plus added kicks that are unique. Fresh and creative archery games found nowhere else are among attractions that account for the rapid blossoming of under-roof facilities all over the map.

Lane operations give first aid to hundreds of beginners smitten with the bow-bug every month. They provide instant answers to those time-honored questions: Where do I go? How do I get started?

Usually the greenhorn arrives at the lanes with no equipment except a feverish desire. The operator furnishes basic tackle from his stock, selecting it carefully to fit the novice's bodily capabilities. Then comes a lesson in shooting form, including safety, under expert tutelage. The latter is assured, since the operator and his staff are professional instructors— very likely certified by the Professional Archers Association.

Inside an hour, the beginner has satisfied his initial cravings. He or she has gotten the feel of proper, good-quality gear through hands-on shooting, and found a gathering-place to be with other denizens of the bow-world. For a modest investment in lane rental and instruction, the individual has taken a seven-league step forward.

"In about three hours of shooting," says Bill Watson, operator of lanes in New Jersey and Pennsylvania, "most newcomers will be slapping arrows into the butt consistently. Then is when they begin thinking about buying their own tailored bows, arrows and accessories. We don't encourage buying until they're sure they've really fallen for the sport."

The booming popularity of the modern lane, with its motorized, movable targets and quick-scoring methods, draws shooters from the entire spectrum of archer interest and experience. In high-spirited, sociable action you'll find a hodge-podge of target specialists—field-style bowmen, hunters, Olympic hopefuls, men and women, boys and girls, and seasoned veterans, as well as rank freshmen.

An amazing variety of events has been devised to keep everybody happy. A key ingredient is the formation of teams and setting up of leagues to assure maximum participation. Alternates are named for the teams to keep matches on schedule when someone fails to show up. Games and targets are tailored to fit short-distance shooting (rarely more than thirty yards). The number of arrows shot and general rules of conduct are gauged to prevent dragged-out contests. Most indoor rounds will engage four bowmen on a single lane hardly more than an hour, from the first shot to the final tally. A typical range has a dozen lanes. A pair of archers can shoot side by side at one target butt.

The routine program of a nearby indoor range gives a glimpse of intense activity. Open seven days a week until 10 P.M., there are leagues for four-shooter teams, two-shooter teams, hunting bowmen, mixed doubles, international metric-round specialists, and beginners. In addition, there's an open league for two-shooter teams using any equipment at all—bare bows, sights, target models, compounds and whatever. Each Saturday morning the place swarms with young folks training in the Junior Olympic Archers Development Class.

A pleasing feature of most league shooting is the use of a handicapping system. In a manner similar to other games, extra points are awarded to individuals, based on their average

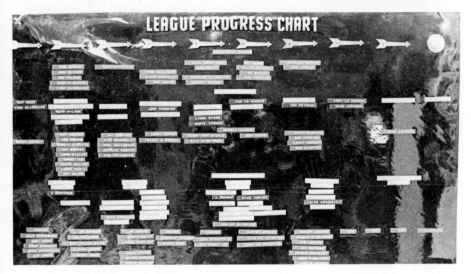

A league progress chart.

scores. The actual number of points "spotted" to a less-skilled archer is a percentage of the difference between the real score and the total possible score.

The method was designed by the American Indoor Archery Association (AIAA) to encourage a more even footing among seasoned bowmen and those new to the sport.

AIAA welcomes new members at any stage of their archery careers. Membership offers an opportunity to shoot for recognized achievement in local, regional and national tournaments. It is also a chance to help support the AIAA's major, highly beneficial efforts. The organization works to bring safer, roomier lanes to the public. Members also promote the invention of livelier, more entertaining games for the bow and arrow —and a brighter place in the sun for archery in general.

Co-operating with these aims is the membership of the Archery Lanes Operators Association (ALOA). The one hundred-plus ranges owned and managed by these archery businessmen are designed to comply with the shooting rules of the AIAA. This includes uniform lane dimensions, target sizes, illumination, height of ceiling and liability insurance. ALOA insists on strict safety standards to protect shooters and spectators, plus a generous number of hours of operation per week.

To be certified by ALOA, range owners must also provide a first-class tackle shop on the premises. This gives the shooting customer a continual education in the latest bow technology— a chance to acquire up-to-date equipment as fast as it hits the market.

The result is that a typical lane operation serves as a kind of informal "academy" of the bow. Relaxed chatting among archers in the refreshment lounge produces valuable swapping of information such as where to go and what to do, critiques of gear used, and how to improve scoring.

An archery-range tackle shop.

This champion archer has just shot a "robin hood"—he split one ar-
row with another.

Operators arrange to feature many "crowd-pleasers." For example, the appearance of a national or world champion, to
demonstrate and give instruction, gives local archers higher
goals to shoot for. Training clinics in the use of more advanced
tackle, such as compound bows, or radical designs in arrow
fletching, are common highlights.

Exhibitions of out-of-the-ordinary tackle might include a
pygmy bow and arrow from the African jungle; or a whip-
ended bow used by traditional Japanese archers; or, again, a
session featuring the lesser-known crossbow. All of the above
items have been presented at indoor lanes in our neighborhood.

Alert range operators furnish entertainment as well as instruction. In addition, indoor events are constantly modified to answer all of the special demands for shooting experience. Examples are the field- and hunting-type rounds devised for the sportsman-archer, including participants in the Fred Bear Indoor League.

Bow-hunter events feature realistic challenges. Animal-silhouette targets are shot at varying distances with genuine game-field tackle. Included are shots made kneeling, crouching and over the shoulder. One inventive operator added a "tree-stand" position for the deer hunters in the crowd.

One of the most imaginative events on the indoor calendar is the SACO Speed Round. This is shot at new-concept targets designed by C. A. (Chuck) Saunders of Columbus, Nebraska. Based on the excitement of high-speed, dead-eye shooting, the Speed Round truly adds a new dimension to archery sports. It's as breathtaking for onlookers to watch as it is for shooters slugging it out in the lanes.

The Saunders target for this event is an upright column holding an arrangement of cups. A pair of cups are mounted, opposite each other, on a metal arm. One cup is orange, the other blue. Hit one cup and it flops out of sight and the opposing cup pivots into view. There are six pairs of cups on a single column. This serves as the common target for each contesting pair of archers.

At the start, each archer in the pair is assigned a color: orange or blue. Facing them, the target column is arranged to expose three orange cups on one side, and three blue cups on the other. The object is to knock those cups over to the opponent's side of the column.

On signal, the bowman-to-bowman "combat" begins. Each has just sixty seconds in which to loose as many sharp-shot arrows as possible. Suspense builds as the clock ticks away and the cups whack back and forth around the column. The crowd is on its feet, breath held, necks craning. Then the cutoff whistle blows and the "low man" wins, by virtue of the *least number* of his color cups exposed. Or a tie may be settled by a twenty-second sudden-death shoot-off.

The game was an instant hit with the crowd at the Desert Inn Archery Classic at Las Vegas, Nevada, where it was introduced by tournament director Joe Johnston. Changes in procedure, such as lengthening the shooting ends to ninety seconds, are still being tested. Winners must triumph over a series of eliminator shoots. In a single tournament they often make two hundred shots in two hours of bow-bending. Light bows are used to prevent fatigue. Heavy models are no advantage for the short, fifteen-yard range.

The cup targets are only 3½ inches in diameter. However, results have shown no edge for sight-shooters over bare-bow contestants. Blunt-headed arrows are required. Hustle is the name of the game. Tackle is adapted for orderly haste, including the use of wide arrow rests, wide nocks and single nocking points. This facilitates quick stringing. Employment of contrasting colors, as one color for the nock and a contrasting color for the string-serving, also accelerates stringing.

Speed Round artists shoot with fast, cool, rhythmic precision. Men and women, boys and girls, compete in the same classes. They are a new breed of champion. For spectators, the game has all the satisfying elements of sound, color, heated action—and instant recognition of what's happening.

Treat yourself to the goings-on at the nearest nest of undercover archers. If you don't find lanes listed in your Yellow Pages, ask a tackle dealer, or drop a line to the organizations mentioned in this chapter.

Targets must be durable.

11. Arrow-stoppers and Target Faces

There is no sadder sight for an archer than the accidental toppling over of a target matt by a high wind or other force. Especially when the matt topples forward and is bristling with high-priced arrows. You, too, will join in the howls of anguish, realizing that a half dozen of your prize shafts are at the bottom of the mess.

We cite this type of accident not because it happens every day, which it doesn't. It simply illustrates the point that what you're shooting *at* must meet necessary standards. The ability to remain upright is just one of these.

The selection of targets and arrow-stopping material will confront you immediately if you intend to set up your own practice range. On joining a club, you're likely to have frequent turns at target-tending, one of the chores shared by everyone.

Stopping the arrow—without danger to life or property—is surely a number-one requirement for any target. This is reason enough to choose and install stopping devices with utmost care.

In addition, the arrow must be halted without damage to itself. It must stick firmly in the target for proper scoring. Yet, the shooter should be able to withdraw it easily.

Durability is a must. A single target will be hit by hundreds of arrows in just one day. For instance, four archers shooting an FITA Round will launch exactly 576 arrows, not counting practice shots. Small wonder that some target units are designed to withstand up to 100,000 shots before replacement.

Two types of arrow-stoppers in general use are matts and butts (or buttresses). The circular-shaped matt is most common to target-style archery. Butts are the upright, massive blocks of materials used on field ranges or other permanent setups, including indoor lanes.

Tightly wound Indian cordgrass, grown wild on prairies of our West, is the material used for one of the more popular target matts. The grass is fine-textured and remarkably tough. It *gives way* to an arrow thrust rather than shattering. When the arrow is withdrawn, the grass fibers snap back to their original tight-weave position. The cordgrass matt takes a beating from thousands of missiles without weakening or coming apart.

A cordgrass matt.

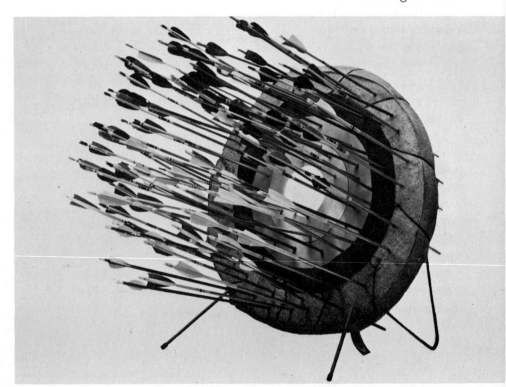

A butt of tightly baled paperboard strips.

Woven and sewn under extreme pressure, cordgrass matts have a density that also makes them rather heavy. Therefore, the smaller, 16-, 24-, and 30-inch models, are most practical for back-yard and other casual uses. For instance, the 30-incher is plenty big for short-range shooting. For shots longer than 30 yards, 36- and 48-inch matts are indicated. Note also that these are a bit awkward to grasp and carry readily.

The prices of high-grade matts may startle you, as they are not cheap. However, dollar for dollar, an investment in superior quality pays off in the long run. Matts made of less serviceable materials deteriorate rapidly. For intensive amounts of shooting, they need frequent replacement and cost more in terms of useful life. In this group are matts made of certain weed grasses; the straw residues of wheat, rye and other grains; and excelsior, which is shredded wood. All have shortcomings as to withstanding abuse, and resisting weather and vermin. Straw, for example, attracts mice.

The heaviest wear, of course, occurs in the central, bull's-eye section. Makers of superior matts, therefore, offer extra cores that may be used to replace or back up severely punctured areas.

Butts and their upkeep are a major budget item on field ranges and indoor lanes. Many indoor-lane operators favor butts of tightly baled paperboard strips presented edgewise to the shooters. Relatively cheap to make and install, they are economical to replace four or five times a year under steady shooting.

At a typical outdoor field range, however, butt maintenance presents a number of problems. A full-scale range setup calls for at least twenty-eight targets and butts scattered over a generally rough area of perhaps twenty acres. Installing them takes considerable work. Once installed, the hefty butts usually must stay put until shot out or weathered to pieces.

Field butts are put to severe testing. They're continually whacked by heavier, hunting-weight arrows. They're subject to wind, rain, snow, drought, freezing and thawing. They're attacked by vermin and by birds in search of nesting materials. Thus, the composition of a field butt is critical.

Salt hay was long ago found to make a superior field butt. It comes from grasses mowed in tidal areas. It is scarce in many parts of the country, and usually expensive where found. Ordinary farm-baled hay and straw are too loosely bound with string to stop an arrow dependably. Excelsior packed in burlap bagging is also ineffective. However, the latter materials, when densely baled with wire or steel tape, will do a fairly adequate job. Field-range clubs are often hard put to find local supplies of bales that meet their specifications. To bridge the gap, they buy baling tools, wire, or metal tape, and package their own butt components as a club project.

Because of their bulk and weight, the larger target matts, and practically all field butts, are left exposed to the elements for long periods. Unprotected, they rot in excessive moisture, or they crumble in prolonged dry spells. Since this means money wasted, wise archers drop slipcovers over their idle target matts. For similar economy, field-rangers usually install roofing paper or other waterproofing on top of their butts. This is mandatory with excelsior, which absorbs water very quickly. Freezing of butts spoils winter shooting because of the high rate of arrow damage.

Secondary backstops for wild arrows are necessary at indoor lanes to prevent shafts from striking and smashing on solid walls. The nylon mesh sheets generally used are expensive. Backstops in the form of old carpets or tarpaulins hung in back of targets may give ample safety protection for home-grounds shooting. Insulation board, two inches thick, will also stop most wild shots and is relatively cheap to buy.

Faces take a lot of punishment.

Faces designed for various shooting events run the gamut in sizes. Official rules dictate the exact sizes: smaller, for close-range shots; larger, for longer ranges. However, all faces are of two general types. One is the bull's-eye with concentric rings. The other is the wildlife silhouette, which sometimes has a ring target printed over it.

Regular target-style archers, indoors or out, always use the ring face. Beginning at the bull and running outward, the colors are yellow, red, blue, black, and white. When divided into ten rings, the zones are scored 10–9–8–7–6–5–4–3–2–1. Junior Olympians shoot the same face divided into five rings with the zones scored 9–7–5–3–1.

The most common face used at indoor lanes in shoots of the American Indoor Archery Association is also ring-target-styled. It is printed in blue with a white dot aiming center, and has five ringed, scoring zones. Values are 5–4–3–2–1, from the center outward.

A ring face.

A wildlife face.

An informal face.

Field-rangers shoot both ringed and wildlife-face targets, depending on the event being shot. The official field round of the National Field Archery Association calls for a black ring surrounding a white bull's-eye, having a black aiming dot at dead center. The outer black scores three. The inner white-plus-dot area scores five. The NFAA hunter round features a square black face with a white aiming center. Again, the outer zone scores three; the inner zone, five. This particular pattern of scoring holds true in virtually all field-type events—that is, five for the central "kill" area; three for the outer "wound" area; and zero for any shot outside the two scoring zones. The wildlife silhouettes are also marked accordingly.

Arrows that break a line between two scoring zones are given the higher-scoring value, without exception, in all target and field events.

For informal "fun and games" there are a host of target choices, readymade on the market, or easily concocted with a little imagination. So if serious practice begins to drag, you might try your bow-and-arrow skills on balloon-busting, tin-can plinking, or games of tic-tac-toe, baseball, poker, etcetera, etcetera.

12. "Tuning" for Accuracy

A prime pleasure of archery is just getting out with other folks who share your interest. The friendly chatter between bowmen advancing around a wooded field course, or shooting it out on a target field, has one central theme. That is, the flight of each arrow shot, why it flew the way it did, why it missed or scored, and ways to make *all* arrows fly right. The search for steady accuracy unites all archers in a common bond. Ever fascinating is the constant popping up of fresh ideas for sharper shooting.

There is no absolutely rigid formula for mastering the bow. A casual glance at a number of archers in action may give the impression that they're all going through the very same motions. But look closely and you'll find that each one is doing something a little bit different.

Check on those little differences. Maybe some of them will work for you. Remember, archery is adventure and recreation. Look for the fun angles. Sure, there are general guides to good shooting form, but don't let them encase you like a suit of armor. Relax and play with your tackle.

The object is to gain control over your equipment, and enjoy doing it. Archers call it "tuning up." Basically, it's a process of adjusting any factor that might affect arrow flight. It involves attending to the function of every item of bow-and-arrow hardware and accessories. It involves the person behind the bow and his technique as parts of the total "shooting machine." Tuning up nears success when an archer knows how his tackle will behave in co-ordination with the best shooting form he can muster.

Many factors bear on sharp or sloppy shooting. One, or several in combination, can influence *arrow clearance.* The idea is to propel the arrow on its path with a minimum of wobbling, gyration or other erratic action. This calls for reducing or eliminating all possible points of friction, dragging or other interference. The various gadgets installed in the sight-window —the shelf, plate, rest, plunger button and so on—attempt to solve the problem of getting the arrow cleanly on its way.

Arrow clearance is also governed by the brace-height of the bow (terms meaning the same are *fistmele* and *string-height*) —that is, the distance between the string and bow measured at the grip when the bow is in the shooting mode. If the brace-height is too shallow, the string may snag or slap your bow-arm. It may also crowd and deflect the arrow as it passes through the window. In either case, arrow clearance will be poor.

A well-equipped sight-window.

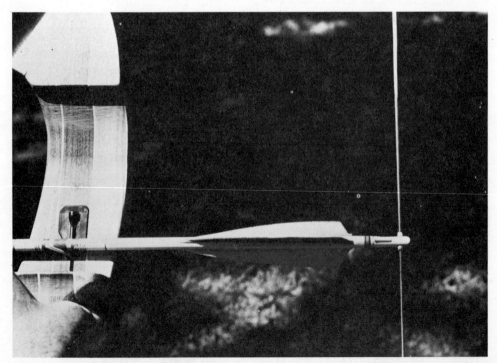

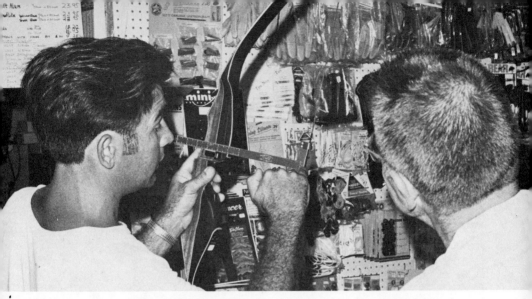

Adjust the brace-height precisely.

Tuning to overcome this is a matter of adjusting brace-height precisely. Fractions of an inch too high, or too low, give quite different results. Generally, you want the lowest string position possible. This position gives maximum thrust. The string will be pushing the arrow for the longest period of time following your release—like the burn of a rocket engine. Another advantage of maximum length of thrust is the few extra split seconds during which the string may lose some of the vibration caused by the release.

It is true that manufacturers often furnish recommended string-heights for bracing each model bow. This helps in choosing the right length for the bowstring, as a starting point for tuning. Figures given should be regarded as averages. They are subject to change, dictated by your experience.

The weight of your arrows, their spine (stiffness or flexibility), their length, type of fletching (feathers, plastic vanes, number of vanes)—all of these factors influence tuning, including variance in brace-height.

You can raise or lower the brace-height simply by twisting the bowstring. Twist it in one direction to loosen the strands and you lower the height. Twist it the other way to tighten the strands; this shortens the string and thus raises the brace-height. Test what this does to shooting at mid-range targets—distances in the 30-, 40- and 50-yard brackets. Keep a record of adjustments and results.

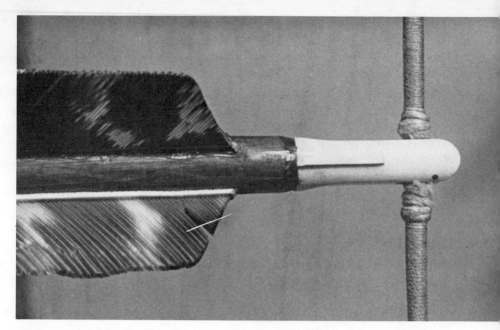

The nocking-point placement is critical.

The nocking-point placement for the arrow is another critical item of tuning. Nearly every archer nocks arrows a trifle higher (⅛ to ³⁄₁₆ inch) than a square angle aligned from bowstring to the arrow rest. Generally, this is to counteract a bouncing effect in the fletching as the shaft slides over the arrow shelf or rest.

Yet, there are champion-caliber archers who place their nocks squarely opposite—neither higher nor lower than—the rest. Still other crack shots nock arrows ⅞ to 1 inch above the horizontal. These bowmen say it brings the arrow closer to the aiming-eye level—cuts down on the margin for aiming error.

Once you detect what occurs when you make a certain alteration, you can use that knowledge for many purposes. For instance, Al Jacobs, a young dentist, is the top instinctive shooter in our own field archery club. Al found that varying his brace-height as little as ¼ inch, and changing his nocking point no more than ¹⁄₁₆ inch, moved his arrows up and down the target as much as six inches. This was at the 40-yard range.

A friend of Al's used this same strategy in winning the Pennsylvania instinctive target crown. The trick that helped him win was simply a measured twisting of his string. He gave ten twists to his string to increase his brace-height. This slowed down his arrows. When shooting 40 yards, he could use the same aiming position as he used at 50 yards. The slowed-down arrows plunked right into the golds.

To calibrate bracing and nocking, a bow-square accessory is needed for fractional adjustments. For setting brace-height alone, however, you can put guide marks on your arrows, or cut off an old arrow to the desired length, or what have you. A good bow-square usually has an added scale to locate the nocking point with precision.

The number of strands in your string may be worth examining and questioning in the course of a tune-up. Although the strand count is generally related to strength of the string needed for the bow's weight, there could be margin for adjustment. Extra, unnecessary strands make for a slower-acting bow and sluggish arrows. Check the possibility.

On the subject of sluggish, slow-flying arrows, no test shows this failing better than long-range shooting. By this we mean 60-, 70-, 80- and 100-yard targets. The common practice field tends to peak out at 50 yards. Arrow flight is therefore very brief, which limits the eye's capacity to observe any peculiarities in arrow behavior.

Due to longer flying time, extreme-range shots can be analyzed visually.

For instance, we recently acquired a beautiful new bow, and arrows (supposedly) spine-matched to it. A first practice session was disappointing. At point-blank range, our arrows plopped in persistently low on the target skirt. We switched to the 80-yarder and were dismayed to see that our shots were nearly spent—dropping like howitzer shells—at the far end of the field.

A friend of ours saw our plight and loaned us some lighter-spined arrows. The improvement was startling. At mid-range and point-blank aim, our arrows moved up to a center-target grouping. And, at downfield far distances, the shafts showed no signs of falling spent. On our next trip to the tackle shop we picked up a sheaf of lighter arrows. Contrary to what the original specifications said, the substitutes have plenty of control and speed at all practical distances we shoot.

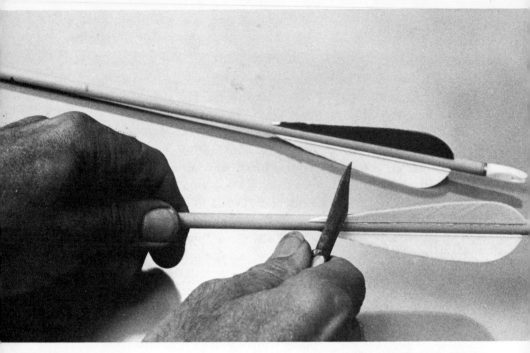

Arranging the fletching.

Another facet of arrow design that may affect tuning is the fletching. The two common materials, feathers and plastic, may call for differing brace-heights and nocking points. This is because they usually differ in resistance as they zip out of the bow. Shape and size of the vanes in the fletching also affect resistance to be reckoned with. Shooters of the newer, compound bows, for example, usually favor shallower ("skinnier") vanes to cut down resistance.

The nock-fitting of the arrow on the string can also be critical. Too loose or sloppy a fitting can impact extra wobbles as the shaft leaves the string. Too tight a pinch can hang up and slow the shot. Here's the test: Nock an arrow and aim the bow at the ground. Remove your string-hand. The shaft should dangle without aid. Give the string a light tap. The arrow should fall off.

Remedies: You have choices. One way is to replace your nocks with those of proper size. Another way is to reduce or build up the string-serving, according to need. Again, certain types of nocks can be softened in hot water, then pinched or spread, as needed.

Dozens of devices are available to provide for best clearance of the arrow's passage through and beyond the bow. Popular devices include arrow rests having tiny arms, or brushes, or nylon wafers that cradle the passing shaft. Increasingly popular with target-shooters is a spring-loaded button rest. The spring can be adjusted to increase or relax tension, which in turn modifies resistance to the arrow, thus offering maximum control in relation to specific arrow designs.

Some archers find that a draw-check installed in the sight-window aids their tuning. The common design is a spring that emits a clicking signal which indicates that you have drawn your shaft full-length. Beware, bare-bow shooters: Any gadget sticking up above the arrow that might provide aiming assistance, could be declared illegal at a competition shoot.

Checking the nock-fitting.

Don't overlook the basic accessories in any zealous tune-up. Nothing is more basic than a good armguard to keep your string from hanging up, and to prevent bruises. Armguards are vital to arrow clearance and should be worn over the naked arm in summer, or over a garment sleeve in cool weather. Short cuff styles and elbow-to-waist models are available, according to coverage needed.

Just as basic is the shooting glove, or shooting tab, if the latter is your preference. Select whichever suits your comfort and permits the cleanest release of the bowstring. The release is at the heart of fine tuning. Therefore, your glove or tab should afford smooth, snag-free slippage the instant your fingers go limp and the string propels the arrow on course.

Users of mechanical sights (free style) will spend considerable time tuning these instruments. Settings of the aiming pin for various distances are determined by a series of test shots and relative corrections to the left or right, up or down. Then the sight-scale is marked to indicate the right location for specific yardages or meters.

Bare-bow shooters do their own type of aim-tuning. Here it should be noted that *aiming* is in fact practiced even *without the use of a sighting gadget*. One method is called "gap" shooting. The idea is to learn and memorize the gap between the arrow tip and the bull's-eye, when aiming over the drawn

Be sure you have a good armguard.

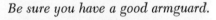
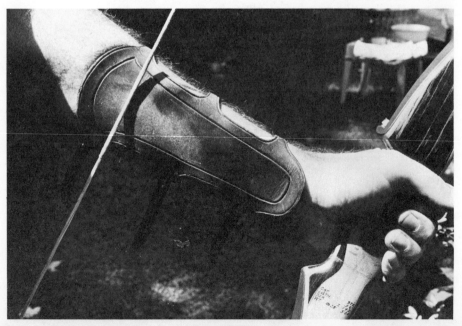

A mechanical sight.

arrow, that will drive the arrow straight home. The gap, of course, changes according to the distance.

Enthusiasts for the bare bow may also "walk the string." In this system the archer may forsake the traditional one-finger-over-and-two-fingers-under grip on the bowstring. Instead, the archer positions his fingers variously up or down the string. The arrow remains at its preset nocking point. The effect is to elevate or depress the alignment of the arrow. The archer's objective is to memorize his fingers' position for each distance shot while at the same time aiming the tip of the arrow directly at the center of the target.

Thus, although bare-bowmen are classified "instinctive," you'll note that the term is not entirely accurate.

A few who shoot in dead-eye fashion, totally "by feel," have amazing prowess. Perhaps the most famous in modern times are Howard Hill and Fred Bear. Both have shown the lightning-fast deadliness of their skill in hunting. In the main, you may be sure a technique of aiming is employed by most bowmen—with or without sights.

The under-chin anchor.

Selecting and holding an exact anchoring spot on your face while aiming is yet another vital part of tuning. The under-chin anchor—with the string just touching nose and mouth—is common with target specialists. Hunters and field-range shooters more often go to a corner-of-mouth or a cheek anchor. Some accomplished shooters will switch from cheek, to mouth, to chin, according to the distance being shot—going to the chin hold for longer ranges.

Note that the lower down you anchor on your face, the higher will be the upward tilt of your arrowhead—and the higher and more distant will the shaft fly.

Experiment to find the spot that gives you the best returns, but line up your string, always, ahead of your aiming eye.

Our friend Al Jacobs, the longbow expert and practicing dentist, applies his medical training to archery tuning-up. "To me, it's about ninety-nine per cent biophysics," says Al. "It's a dual effort to blend your human machinery with the hardware machinery of your tackle. When they're working in absolute harmony, then you get on-the-beam accuracy."

The cheek anchor.

Tuning the body means disciplining it to perform all the co-ordinated motions of launching an arrow with unwavering good form. That includes the way you stand, address the target, extend and hold the bow, draw, anchor with locked *back tension*, aim, release, and follow through.

Perhaps the least-understood and hardest-to-explain element of body-tuning is back tension. It may take months, even years, to master, as a "secret" of the complete archer.

Drawing the bow.

Pay attention to your back tension.

Mastery of back tension begins with the method of drawing the arrow. Instead of your arm, use your more powerful back muscles to pull back the bowstring. The arm, thus, behaves as a rigid rod hooked to the string. At full length of the draw, when properly executed, you'll feel back muscles arrive at a natural stop. You'll sense its comfort along with an ease in holding the draw while you aim. Releasing the arrow then becomes a leisurely, passive motion. There is no conscious unfolding of the string-fingers. Rather, you just relax your back. The relaxation trickles down your arm to the string, and away goes your arrow on a silken-smooth launch.

A mechanical release.

The archery industry offers an ample array of materials and mechanical aids for tuning for the highest degree of accuracy. A wide selection of sighting devices is available to meet almost every aiming problem encountered by the targeteer, field-range devotee, or hunter. All manner of torque stabilizers and counterweights are at hand, generally designed to steady the bow—prevent it from bouncing around and delivering a wobbly arrow.

If one has trouble maintaining a uniform grip on the bow, there's a "bow-positioner" remedy. To control the anchor, there's the commonly seen kisser. When drawn to the mouth, this little wafer device assures a precise aiming location for every shot.

Sighting-aid users will find a choice of rear sights in the form of peepholes that may be installed in the string.

For those seeking the ultimate in smooth arrow releases, there are a dozen or more mechanical-type releases as substitutes for the ordinary finger methods. They are restricted in official competition.

Archers should bear in mind that the use of various material aids may limit their qualification to shoot in specific events. Check the official rule books when in doubt.

However far you go in your tuning-up process, let it be one of fun-filled discovery. Go at it one step at a time. It's all a matter of patiently getting acquainted with your tackle—of becoming comfortable and happy with it. You've arrived when the bow and you are as one.

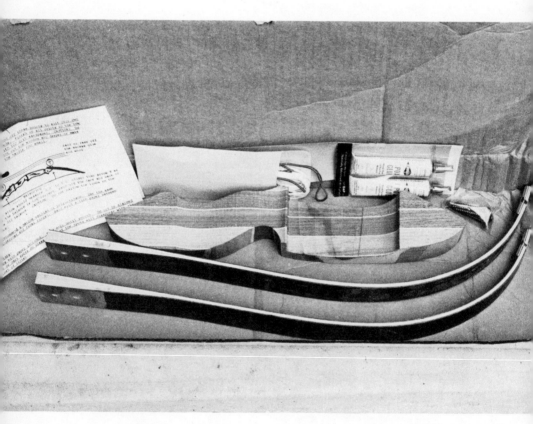

A bow kit.

13. The Complete Archer

Most of us are a far cry from the long-ago Indian boy or medieval yeoman who made bows and arrows from scratch with his own two hands.

Thanks to a thriving industry, we're no longer forced to chop bow-staves out of the forest, fashion strings of plant fiber or animal sinew, select reeds for shafts, catch birds for feather fletching, or chip arrowheads out of flint stone.

Today, there's a treasure of readymade tackle at hand, plus an increasing number of archer-technicians qualified to give advice. Still, we recommend that you work toward a measure of independence. There are a range of things you can make, install, repair, adjust or acquire. They'll give you the satisfaction of standing pretty much on your own two feet.

Following are suggestions aimed to make you a more self-reliant archer.

It's possible to assemble a bow from kits offered by several suppliers. Try it if you have the tools, and if you've done other wood and plastic projects successfully. A typical bow kit requires you to attach the two limbs to the central riser section. This is done by means of lag screws and cement. The limbs must be trimmed—gradually and carefully—for perfect tillering. This means equal bend and strength in each limb.

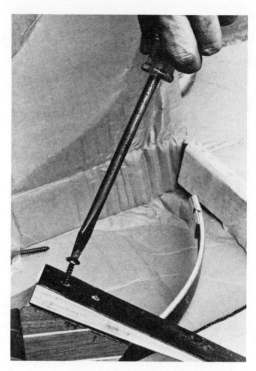

Attach the two limbs to the central riser section.

Then you must rasp, file and sand the rough surface of the riser blank, to give smooth beauty to the sight-window, arrow shelf and grip. Several coats of varnish, with sanding between coats, provide a final finish. Nocks and grooves are trimmed out of the bow-tips to accept the string loops. Finally the bowstring is installed, also an arrow plate and rest, and you're ready to shoot.

The kit will cost about 20 per cent less than a comparable finished bow bought off the rack, not counting the time you spend on the project. Assembly and finish will take six or seven days, including periods for cement and varnish to dry. Your reward, however, can be a bow customed exactly to your taste, plus a gut feeling of accomplishment.

File the rough surface of the riser blank.

The finished bow.

Arrow-clearance devices are generally easy to install in the sight-window. These are such items as shelf mats, arrow plates and arrow rests. Most are provided with sticky backs and are simply pressed into place. The arrow rest, for example, should be emplaced so that the shaft passes one-half inch above the shelf. Any gadgetry that calls for screw- or bolt-mounting should be approached with caution. Unless the bow already has special fittings, drilling or cutting may weaken it. Get an expert opinion beforehand.

Knowledge of bowstrings is a key element in shooting. First of all, buy an extra string immediately. Carry it afield at all times. Take your original string to the dealer to insure a perfect match. If your bow was made to modern AMO standards, the AMO specifications inscribed on the handle will indicate the correct string. In this case, a string three inches shorter than your bow-length will afford the right brace-height and strength.

A double-loop (meaning a loop at each end) string will have one loop larger than the other. The small loop goes into the lower-limb nock, allowing the larger loop to slide up or down the upper limb as the bow is braced or unbraced.

A single-loop string may be installed by tying a timber-hitch knot attached to the nock of the lower limb.

Signs of string wear show earliest in the serving material at the central arrow-nocking place and likewise at the end loops. You can replace the servings with little difficulty yourself. You can wind the material on by hand; but an inexpensive serving spool does a better, neater job. Use cotton or twisted nylon thread for end servings. For the center serving, you can choose between stranded cotton and nylon, monofilament nylon, and Teflon monofilament. We prefer nylon mono. It gives a slick release for the arrow, and it can be sanded to a nice fit for the arrow nock.

Examine the entire length of your string regularly. If any of the main strands have frayed or parted, replace the entire string before you get hurt.

In use, a new string will stretch as much as ½ to ¾ inch. This of course will lower the brace-height. Twist, to bring it

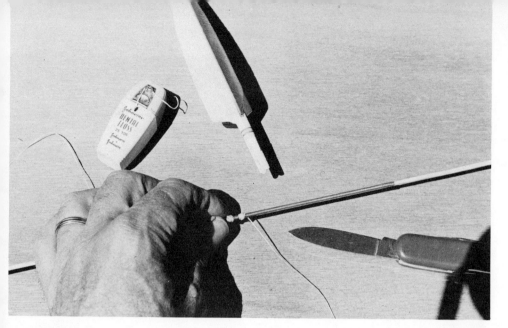

Replacing the servings.

back to normal. Overtwisting will weaken it. Shortening by ½ inch in this manner will raise the brace-height by about ¾ inch, which is usually ample leeway.

Making arrows of superior quality requires precision equipment and top craftsmanship. However, many archers meet the challenge halfway. They buy mill-length shafts already fletched. Then they cut them to their own specs and install the heads, nocks, and cresting themselves. This provides some savings plus satisfaction. There is little economy in home arrowsmithing unless supplies are bought in bulk—preferably in units of one hundred or more.

Some hobbyists take advantage of bulk rates by "chipping in" and sharing a large order of materials. Care should be taken to specify such items as correct spine, shaft diameter, right- or left-spiral fletching and so on. A feather-burner to shape the vanes will be needed, unless the vanes are bought already die-cut. A precision model jig to install each vane is another must. To speed up the fletching process, several jigs are required. This permits working on more than a single arrow at a time.

Special tools are also desirable in order to do a tidy job of cutting fiberglass and aluminum shafts to proper length.

Arrows of superior quality are difficult to make.

A jig is needed to install each vane.

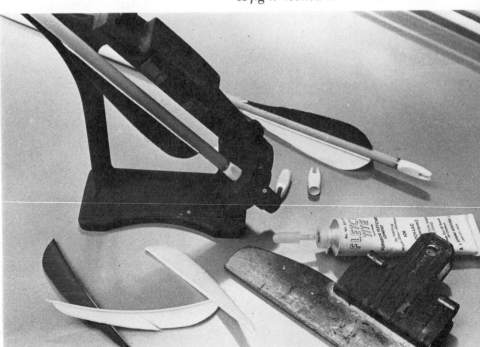

The jig in use.

Cementing is critical.

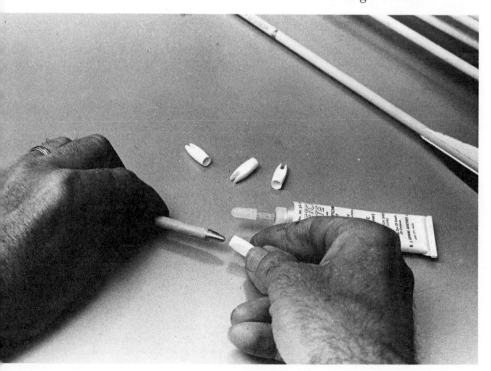

An ordinary sharp hobby knife can be used to trim off wooden shafting. The trick is to roll the shaft, making a shallow cut all the way around, so that it will snap in two with a little pressure, leaving a few center fibers to be trimmed off clean.

Wood shafts generally must be tapered to accept points and nocks. A special tool, like a pencil sharpener, is used.

Insert fittings are typical of glass and aluminum, due to their hollow tubing.

Cementing is the critical operation in arrow-making and repair. You'll recognize this as soon as poorly cemented parts begin to vanish from the shaft. There are many excellent adhesives designed to cling solidly to the various shaft materials. Each requires careful attention to the bonding surfaces on which they're used.

Cementing techniques for glass and wood are similar. Surfaces to be bonded should be solid and dirt-free.

Aluminum, because it is a metal, needs specific preparation. Conditioning methods before fletching include scrubbing the aluminum with a nondetergent cleanser, followed by rinsing with warm, distilled water, and drying. A special acid dip can be substituted for the cleanser. Another method is to lightly sand the fletch area with fine grit paper, followed by wiping on a lacquer thinner. Fletching is affixed with special cement designed for use with metals.

Whatever the material, recommended drying times for successful bonding must be strictly observed. Placement of nocks, points and vanes needs to be gnat's-eyebrow accurate. A misaligned nock, for example, will throw an arrow off flight path. Remember, too, the groove in the nock has to be set at right angles to the cock vane.

The colored, quick-dry lacquers found in hobby shops can be used to stripe on cresting for wood and glass arrows. Automotive-type lacquers must be used on aluminum. Again, the areas painted must be clean and otherwise prepared for good bonding of the crest.

Any archer with a penchant for leathercraft will discover many projects for this skill. Armguards, shooting tabs, quivers, belts, belt cases, bow-slings and chest protectors are among the more useful suggestions. An accomplished leather-worker can make these ornamental, too.

A popular leather project is a quiver, in kit form, marketed by many craftwork stores. The design will hold a half-dozen or more target arrows, and has a separator to protect the fletchings. Also, the craftsman has the choice of rigging it to wear over the shoulder, or slung from a belt.

The clever hobbyist, with proper tools, may elect to carve the cowhide with any sort of ornamental figures in relief. Another might choose to embellish it with designs or scenes painted or dyed in permanent, weatherproof colors. Again, the quiver could be decorated with attractive beadwork such as American Indian motifs. In any case, the artwork would be applied to leather in the flat, before assembling.

Homemade leather equipment.

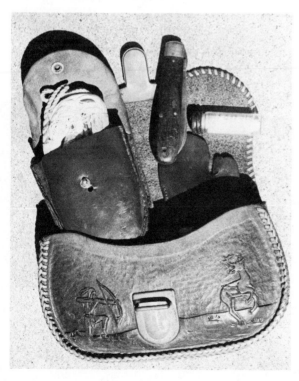

A quiver kit.

Decorating the quiver.

Completing the quiver includes cementing an inner liner to the main piece of cowhide; sewing, cementing and lacing all of the joined edges; cementing in the bottom piece; and finally riveting on the straps used to suspend the quiver on the archer's person. An average craftsman will spend about a week of rewarding concentration on this project. The time involved will depend on the amount of embellishment. Without the elegance, however, the quiver is still serviceable.

Every quiver should be equipped with a tassel. The gadget has a fancy look, but its true utility is for wiping arrows free of mud and other field debris. Make one yourself by first acquiring a handful of yarns about a foot long. Double the yarns into a bell-shaped tassel and bind with a length of nylon or other stout cord. Fluff out the yarns, and there you have it.

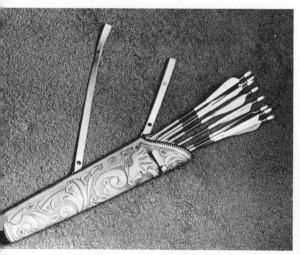

The result.

The quiver tassel.

Knowing which items to take on, and which to skip, is the hallmark of the complete, self-sufficient archer. Experience in the particular brand of shooting you prefer will give you the best guidance. Yet, a few basic aids are important to every archer's kit.

Aside from elementary shooting gear, the following objects will be handy to have with you. They'll fit into your quiver and small belt case, and leave room for a sandwich:

Bowstringer—The safest way to brace the bow. Try before buying one. All types do not fit all bows.

Bow-boots—They slip over and protect bow-tips.

String-keeper—A device that snugs the string to the bow when unbraced. It keeps the string from falling off or snagging.

Beeswax—Carry a lump to rub on the string now and then for weatherproofing and conditioning.

Extra bowstring—First, try it on the bow, install the nocking point, shoot a dozen or more arrows to stretch it. Take the string off and carry it in reserve.

String maintenance material—Include a spool of proper thread to repair servings, dental floss to install a tie-on type of nocking point, or an extra unit of the slip-on or crimp-on style of nock locator.

Brace-height checker—This may be a bow-square, or simply an arrow marked to indicate the correct brace-height of your bow.

Extra arrows—Let's face it, they do break indoors. Outdoors, they break and also get lost. At a minimum, take along spares equivalent to two or three more than the kind of "end" you'll be shooting. Examples: for a six-arrow end, bring along eight or nine; for a four-arrow end, take six or seven; and so on. Adjust the figure up or down according to your known ability to hit the butt every time.

Arrow-upkeep material—Pack one or two extra points, nocks, fletch vanes, and suitable cements. Field repairs may keep you shooting when your first-line arrows suffer damage.

Tools—Most first-aid jobs can be handled with this kit: a small, sharp jackknife; miniature fine-toothed file; piece of fine-grain emery paper; surgical tape; small pair of pliers; write-on-anything felt pen, to mark measurements, etc.

The above list is trimmed down to handy and frequent necessities. It can be amplified according to specialized needs and desires. For instance, serious target archers might add tackle boxes and spotting scopes. And field-range shooters might think of brush-buttons, bow-quivers, binoculars and so on.

A final consideration for the complete archer is safekeeping valuable tackle around the house. Arrangements can be as elaborate as assigning an entire cabinet to contain all of your bows and gadgetry. Or, simply use of an area of the basement or workshop to rack and consolidate your armament out of harm's way.

Wherever your storage area, make sure the atmosphere isn't overmoist, or overheated and ultra dry. Cementing materials, plastics, woods, leathers and feathers all suffer from extremes of temperature and humidity.

Let's not sally forth with a cracked bow—or arrows with worm-eaten fletching.

Store your tackle carefully.

14. Olympics Fever

In modern Olympic Games, dating back to 1896, archery is the "sport that refused to die." Archers took the field of honor and were acclaimed with other athletes in 1900, 1904, 1908 and 1920. Then the sport was dropped under a ruling which stated that "it was not widely practiced in at least twenty-five countries." Thereafter, a whole generation was born and grew up unaware that Olympic bowmen had ever existed.

As bow-sport began climbing back to favor after World War II, enthusiasts struggled to restore its former glory. They finally won over the Olympic Committee by showing worldwide strength in archer organization.

At the twentieth Summer Olympic Games in Munich, Germany, in 1972, archery reappeared in the front rank of twenty-three hotly contested sports. The long-awaited event was due largely to vigorous promotion by leaders of the International Archery Federation. This body is commonly known by its French name, Fédération Internationale de Tir à l'Arc. FITA now speaks firmly on behalf of national archer groups in over fifty Olympic-affiliated countries. New archer-nations join Federation ranks continually.

The symbolic first-place gold medals in both the Ladies' and Gentlemen's divisions at Munich were won by the U.S.A. Several other countries were only a few arrow hits behind. Archers of the Soviet Union, East Germany, West Germany, Poland, England, Canada, Australia and the Scandanavian nations have since shown rapid improvement. Scores now registered by top shooters in every competing country indicate coming "battles of the giants" in future Oympiads.

Many a top-rank archer has revealed that he or she began by "just fooling around with the bow—and suddenly deciding to get serious with it." This could happen to you, whatever your present level of interest. If you get swept away by Olympic fervor, you'll be interested in the process of being named to a U.S. team. Following are some of the steps toward that goal.

First of all, note that the Olympics are strictly for amateur sportsmen and sportswomen. You must never have received any form of pay from your sport, either directly or indirectly. You need also to realize the spirit of the Olympics. The games are not planned as contests between countries. They're aimed to inspire good will among individual sportsmen in fair contest, who may thus spread friendship across international boundaries and between their respective nations.

All Olympic archers are governed by precise international (FITA) rules as to equipment and shooting conduct. Tackle regulations are spelled out at length. In brief, bows must be conventional. No compound types are allowed. Sighting devices may have no special optics such as glass prisms or magnifiers. String peepsights are out. There is a limit on the size of torque-compensating weights affixed to the bow. No mechanical arrow releases are permitted; finger releases only, is the rule.

No distinction is made between free-stylers and instinctive shooters under present Olympic regulations. Therefore, the use of aiming aids is universal in practice, for their proven advantage over the bare bow.

Competitors prepare themselves and their equipment specifically for the official Olympic archer's round. This is the rugged FITA Round with a total of 144 arrows: 36 arrows shot at each of four different distances. Men shoot at 90, 70, 50 and 30 meters. Women shoot at 70, 60, 50 and 30 meters. In both

The FITA emblem.

cases, the target-face size is 122 centimeters for the two longer ranges; and 80 centimeters for the two shorter ranges.

Two complete FITA Rounds are shot over a period of several days at standard ten-ring targets. Ring values are scored 10–9–8–7–6–5–4–3–2–1, beginning at the center gold bull's-eye. The totals scored for the two rounds determine the Olympic winners. In case of tie scores, the decision goes to the archer scoring the greater number of hits on the scoring zones.

Long before an archer is entitled to wear the colorful blazer and crest signifying membership in the U. S. Olympic squad, he and she will have triumphed over many a long day's shooting. To reach the final tryouts, each hopeful must shoot four qualifying scores in a ten-month period.

A single FITA Round of 144 arrows, all solidly in the bull's-eye, would produce 1,440 points. Therefore, a qualifying minimum for men is 1,100 points. For women, it is 1,050, a scant difference of 5 perfectly shot arrows.

Final tryouts for the squad are shot hardly more than a month before the Games. This crucial test is an authentic replica of the actual Olympics—the same rounds, metric distances and rigid FITA rules of conduct. The relative handful of finalists are already champions, or they wouldn't have gotten this far. Still to be proven is whether they can stand the pressure from brilliant bowmen recruited from every corner of the globe.

A member of the Junior Olympic Archers Development Program.

As suspense-laden hours of shooting come to an end, three men and three women stand out at the final score-posting. They will carry U.S. colors and hopes into the upcoming Olympic arena. Both men and women will very likely have shot better than 1,200-point FITA single rounds.

At the time of this writing, Darrell Pace of the U.S.A. holds the world's record FITA for men, at 1,291 points. Emma Gapchenko of the U.S.S.R. holds the record for women, with 1,235.

To insure a steady supply of talent for U.S. teams, a Junior Olympic Archers Development Program is operating in all fifty states. This is directed by the National Archery Association to give expert instruction, good facilities and incentive for young shooters up to eighteen years of age. Thousands of boys and girls get their start in JOAD at camps, schools, indoor and outdoor ranges each year. Aside from Olympic interests, NAA thus supports our national goals of physical fitness and a healthy lifetime sport pursuit for all U.S. citizens.

Through JOAD's incentive process, local archery lanes have become recreational action centers for neighborhood youth. Shooting one or two hours a week at reduced rates with rented tackle, youngsters master the gradually stepped-up achievement skills with amazing speed. Eight progressive rankings are Yeoman, Junior Bowman, Junior Archer, Bowman, Archer, Master Archer, Expert Archer, and Olympic Archer.

Yeoman rank, for example, requires a minimum score of 60 points for 30 arrows shot into a 36-inch target at 15 yards. At the top end of the scale, the Olympic rank requires a minimum score of 260 for 30 arrows aimed at a 16-inch target on a range of 20 yards. The standard face is the familiar gold-red-blue-black-white concentric-ring design. For JOAD, it is scored as five zones—9, 7, 5, 3, and 1—beginning with the gold bull.

Junior Olympic shoot-offs are frequently scheduled as features of national and regional championships held for senior archers. Spectator interest bubbles over when the young folks step to the shooting line. Although classed in three age groups as under twelve, twelve to fifteen, and fifteen to eighteen, the junior event is otherwise a lively free-for-all. Girls shoot it out, toe to toe, with the boys; sighters match arrows with the bare-bow purists; good-natured but "no-fooling" rivalry prevails.

Out of such high-spirited contests and the JOAD program-at-large, members of the new generation of archers are lifting bow-skills to heights thought impossible a very few years ago. When future Olympians receive their gold, silver and bronze medal awards, ex-JOADs are very likely to be among those honored.

Cocking the crossbow.

15. "Cousin" Crossbow

Consider here the longbow's closest "relative" in the family of archery weapons. Attach a typical bent-stick-with-string to a typical gunstock-with-trigger, and you have a crossbow—and romance known to comparatively few shooters.

Organized crossbow archers number scarcely five hundred enthusiasts in the U.S.A. Firsthand insight on their experience is all the more interesting to discover.

"Yes, the crossbow does have an evil image in the eyes of most people, as they think of it as a powerful and therefore dangerous weapon. Many visualize a crossbow as made from an automobile leaf-spring, requiring a block and tackle or some sort of jack or winch to cock the thing. Such weapons are novelties and are not seen in competition."

The foregoing is the comment of a seasoned crossbowman answering one of our questions. Gil Frey, corresponding secretary of the National Crossbowmen of the U.S., confirmed our hunch that there is indeed a sort of prejudice lingering on, particularly in America. Perhaps there've been too many movies depicting crossbowmen as low-browed, lumbering villains taking unfair advantage of cheerful, chivalrous, clever and always heroic longbowmen.

Whatever the reason, Gil Frey asserted that today's crossbow fans have a strong alliance with users of "regular" tackle. The National Crossbowmen, in fact, shoot alongside longbowmen in tournaments sponsored by the National Archery Association. The two breeds do not compete against each other. Crossbow marksmen shoot the NAA Rounds, but use a half-size (24-inch diameter) target. Even so, they run up scores comparing closely with those for the longbow.

As further evidence of accuracy, a good crossbowman is expected to place most of his shots inside a 4.8-inch bull's-eye from a distance of 40 yards.

Frey told us: "Our arrows are roughly half the length of longbow arrows, and may be of wood, fiberglass or aluminum tubing, with feathers, or plastic vanes, and have no nocks. Bows must be *hand-drawn only,* and are usually of solid or laminated fiberglass. They pull between 50 and 80 pounds at draws from 16 to 20 inches, producing arrow velocities over 200 feet per second."

In those few states that permit public hunting with the crossbow, models used for large game will pull at 100 pounds and more. Even heavier-weight units appear at "flight shooting" (long-distance) contests. The all-time record crossbow flight-shot is over 2,000 yards—considerably more than a horizontal mile.

Crossbowery has strong appeal for the do-it-yourself craftsman. Although readymade tackle is gradually improving, few of the units marketed satisfy experienced advocates of the sport. Most crossbows seen afield will have been customed by their owners in home workshops. Many are fine examples of woodworking art, as well as scientific design. A wide choice of performers is available in plans developed by the sport's numerous experimenters. There are pistol types, military models, big- and small-game hunting designs, cavalry specials, and even repeaters for rapid-fire shooting.

Sights for crossbows span the gamut of sophistication from simple "iron" sights to multipower telescopes with cross-hair reticules.

Veteran crossbowman Gil Frey says: "We're gaining recruits who like to taste all kinds of archery. The crossbow requires

A woodworker's dream.

many of the same techniques as the regular bow—a steady hand, a sharp eye, and co-ordinated breathing and muscle control. However, a crossbowman can become sharp and stay sharp, with somewhat less practice."

Two active crossbow groups welcome members from any part of the United States. They are: The National Crossbowmen (Thomas Hock, president, 7100 Euclid Road, Cincinnati, Ohio 45248), and The American Crossbow Association (Georges Stevens, founder and director, P. O. Box 72, Huntsville, Arkansas 72740). The former concentrates on a calendar of target contests held around the U.S.A. The latter promotes the sport of crossbow-hunting, and holds a colorful demonstration at Huntsville every year during the second week of October.

Aiming the crossbow.

Crossbow enthusiasm runs high in Europe, where there are highly developed shooter organizations in the Lowland Countries, Sweden, England and Ireland. The British Crossbow Society sponsors international matches by mail. Other international contests are held at various locations—often in conjunction with championship events for longbow archers.

16.   Archer's Information Directory

Hundreds of thousands of men, women and children cross the threshold into the archer's world each year with millions of questions on their minds.

Each question deserves a special answer, tailored to the individual who asks. That's because everyone who steps up to the shooting line is different from all other shooters. The individual is "king" in archery.

Basic principles of getting started with proper equipment and sound techniques are covered in this book. A few months of steady, serious practice on the range leads most new archers to one all-important discovery. The discovery is—how infinitely much more they need to know.

The more one shoots—trying various tackle, ranges and locations—the keener grows the desire to increase knowledge.

If you, as a beginner, have reached a stage of bursting curiosity, regard it as a healthy sign. It simply means you've gained enough experience to recognize the unknowns. Veterans of long years with the bow will encourage you to heed your every urge to challenge traditional methods, seek extra bits of advice, and try the untried. The spectacular continuing advance of archery, even as you read this book, proves the merit of this attitude.

An immediately satisfying way to strengthen your store of know-how is to seek the company of other archers. As a group, they are among the most communicative of all sportsmen. Show the slightest interest in an average bowman's equipment or style and you'll set off an instant exchange of ideas. The old weapon disciplines shooters to be ever alert for fresh points of view. So venture an opinion, solicit comments, watch for helpful hints—out on the range, in the clubhouse, among your fellow customers at the pro tackle shop. You'll be rewarded.

Reading, as you are now, will surely deepen your understanding of the sport. Books on archery aren't numerous, compared with other subject areas. Very few public libraries are overstocked with archery books. Your local library catalogs archery under nonfiction, social science and history—number

Seek the company of other archers.

799.3 in the Dewey decimal system. A large city library may have twenty to thirty different titles. Give the alcoves a try, for fuller appreciation of archery's role in events that shaped the world of today.

Recommended reading, too, are the half-dozen or more national and regional archery magazines, listed at the end of this chapter. Some of the larger "outdoor" magazines also conduct bow-interest departments. They're a means of keeping you alert to new equipment, shooting records, trends in technique and important experiences of bow-people around the globe. Their editors and advertisers are usually willing to correspond with anyone who writes for advice.

Still another live source of helpful current information is represented by the American Archery Council. Its membership is made up of organizations speaking for virtually every type of interest affecting the sport, the shooter and the supporting industry and services.

Acting as a body, the AAC conducts programs to protect archery's welfare and growth as an attractive activity throughout the American community. Its four major campaigns at the moment include: outdoor conservation education for the nation's schools, archery instructor training for physical-education teachers, public understanding of the use of the bow for hunting purposes, and the development of an Archery Hall of Fame.

The names of those thus far inducted into the Hall of Fame read like a roll call of the men and women who have pulled archery out of the dustbin and made it a first-rank modern sport for everyone. A study of their careers will give anyone a better background to understand the gear and shooting methods used today. Established in 1972, the Hall of Fame is located in the Fred Bear Archery Museum at Grayling, Michigan. A few nominees are voted in each year. Each one is memorialized by a plaque, citation and photographs. Honored to date are:

MAURICE THOMPSON: Founder of the National Archery Association in 1879. Through his many books and magazine articles he brought archery to millions of readers throughout the United States and the world.

BEN PEARSON: A leader in the manufacture of archery tackle for more than forty years, he gave unselfishly of his time, money, and talent to promote the sport he loved.

HOWARD HILL: Known as "Mr. Archery" to the world for more than a quarter of a century, his movies and exhibitions gave the sport of archery to millions.

FRED BEAR: His pioneering development of modern archery equipment and manufacturing techniques is matched only by his worldwide contributions to the art of bowhunting.

KARL PALMATIER: His quiet strength and patient guidance as a leader in organized effort has contributed immeasurably to the growth of archery in this country for nearly half a century.

ANN WEBER HOYT: For twenty years the greatest all-round archer in the United States, having won the NAA championships in 1940, 1946, 1947, 1952, and 1953, the NFAA championship in 1955, and the international target and field championship in 1959.

RUSS HOOGERHYDE: Few archers have dominated the sport to the extent he did from 1930 to 1940, winning the NAA championships in 1930, 1931, 1932, 1937, and 1940.

DR. ROBERT ELMER: A six-time National Target Champion. The late Dr. Elmer was author of *Archery and Target Archery*.

RUBE POWELL: Winner of the National Free Style Field Championship five times, while never finishing less than third, from 1951 through 1958.

CLAYTON SHENK: Former president of the National Archery Association, now serving as executive secretary of the organization. Shenk played an important part in the return of archery to the Olympics after an absence of over fifty years. The U.S.A. won both the men's and women's gold medals in Munich in 1972.

DR. SAXTON POPE: The "Father of Modern Bowhunting," Dr. Pope wrote *Hunting with the Bow and Arrow* and *Adventurous Bowman* in the 1920s. His partner, the late Art Young, bagged the first Kodiak bear ever to fall to a modern American bowman. In their honor the Pope and Young Club was organized to keep track of top hunting trophies taken by archers and is recognized the world over.

ART YOUNG: As mentioned in connection with Dr. Pope.

HARRY DRAKE: The most outstanding flight-shooting champion of this century. For more than twenty-five years Harry Drake and Drake flight bows have dominated this archery event.

JAMES (DOUG) EASTON: Devoted nearly a half century of his life to the promotion of archery. Easton pioneered and perfected the aluminum arrow, which today is used almost exclusively in all competitive archery.

JOHN YOUNT: Devoted more than a quarter century of his life to the promotion and administration of the National Field Archery Association.

DOROTHY SMITH CUMMINGS: Winner of the National Archery Association championship seven times from 1919 to 1931, and the Eastern Archery Association eleven times.

Aside from its nationwide projects geared to solve major problems and to widen the sport's recognition, the American Archery Council serves also as a bowman's communications network. Its member organizations are in touch with all archer interests, from the designing board to the shooting line.

For instance, the *Archery Manufacturers Organization* (*AMO*) advances standards in the fabrication of bows, arrows and accessories. They promote high quality and respond to shooters' demands for good, uniform tackle, and constant improvement.

The *Archery Lanes Operators Association* (*ALOA*), in its own words, "unites lane operators into one unit working uniformly and effectively for the development of indoor archery on a commercial basis." ALOA makes and enforces strict rules to insure that its certified lanes are safe, comfortable and within competitive regulations. It also provides directories of lanes available for indoor enthusiasts all over the U.S.A.

Soaring popularity of shooting lanes brought about the *American Indoor Archery Association* (*AIAA*). Parallel to sports such as bowling and golf, this group has established uniform "games" and rules governing indoor team and league competition. This includes a handicap system to take care of less experienced bowmen, differences in age and sex and other inequalities. The association also aims to insure that new members are given first-rate instruction at indoor facilities.

The oldest and most influential alliance for amateurs in the sport is the *National Archery Association of the U.S.A. (NAA).* Through regional and local representatives it sanctions and regulates contests deciding major championships and titles recognized in all phases of archery. NAA rules on archer qualifications and the legality of equipment used in each type of event. As the official sponsoring body for U.S. archers in Olympic competition, NAA is also instrumental in selecting the coaches and members of U. S. Olympic archery teams.

An insigne depicting an old stump with an arrow lodged in it symbolizes the roving/hunting activities promoted by the *National Field Archery Association of the U.S.A. (NFAA).* This large and growing group regulates field-range competition and works to foster wild-game conservation and sportsmanship related to use of the bow and arrow.

Career-oriented bowmen and bow-women are banded together in the *Professional Archers Association (PAA).* These are true enthusiasts who make a living, in full or in part, from

The emblem of the National Field Archery Association of the U.S.A.

teaching archery, putting on demonstrations, performing services, selling equipment, making archery hardware, shooting for prize money, etc. They are creating worthy vocations of commercial bow-activities, paralleling other professional sports. Membership in PAA requires high qualifications, including a year of apprenticeship.

Tailor-made for anyone with high interest in hunting and fishing with bow and arrow is the *Professional Bowhunters Society*. In spite of the name, this group is *not* commercial. It insists on professional-caliber skills and equipment in taking game and fish. Membership applications are carefully screened to admit experienced archers with proven success, particularly on big-game species.

A special division of the NAA worthy of note is the *National Crossbowmen of the U.S.A.* This is a lively and expanding group of devotees. Their aim is to perpetuate, foster and direct the practice of crossbow archery in accordance with official rules and the traditions of this ancient sport.

The following list has been compiled to help you trace any avenue of archery curiosity or pressing need for information to its logical source:

DIRECTORY

PERIODICALS

Archery World—534 North Broadway, Milwaukee, WI 53202

Archery Magazine—Route 2, Box 514, Redlands, CA 92373

Bow & Arrow—Box HH, Capistrano Beach, CA 92624

Bowhunter Magazine—P. O. Box 5377, Fort Wayne, IN 46805

The Big Sky—Rural Route One, Grayling, MI 49738

ORGANIZATIONS

American Archery Council—618 Chalmers St., Flint, MI 48503

Archery Manufacturers Organization—same address as AAC

Archery Lanes Operators Assn.—1500 N. Chatsworth St., St. Paul, MN 55117

American Indoor Archery Assn.—P. O. Box 174, Grayling, MI 49738

National Archery Association—1951 Geraldson Drive, Lancaster, PA 17601

National Field Archery Assn.—Rt. 2, Box 514, Redlands, CA 92373

Professional Archers Assn.—G-6299 Fenton Rd., Flint, MI 48507

Professional Bowhunters Society—P. O. Box 35, Oceola, OH 44860

Fred Bear Sports Club—Rural Route One, Grayling, MI 49738

The National Crossbowmen—3658 Epworth Ave., Cincinnati, OH 45211

Index

BERNHARD A. ROTH, former editor of a leading sportsmen's magazine, has been a freelance writer for many years, concentrating on travel, outdoor recreation, and conservation. He is chief public information officer serving the Northeast and Caribbean areas for the United States Department of Agriculture Soil Conservation Service. An ardent archer, he is also a veteran of motorcycling on three continents, a sailplane pilot, and a member of the Outdoor Writers of America. He is married with three children and lives in a suburb of Philadelphia. Mr. Roth is also the author of *The Complete Beginner's Guide to Motorcycling.*